Live Fully!

Praise for *The Wealth Creator's Playbook*

"*The Wealth Creator's Playbook* offers critical insights and advice that will make life happier and more fulfilling for anyone climbing the ladder of success."
—**Marshall Goldsmith, *New York Times* #1 Best-Selling Author of *Triggers*, *Mojo*, and *What Got You Here Won't Get You There***

"Christianson's 'playbook' for wealth creators is an eminently practical and enlightened guide to understanding our relationship to money, the relationship of money to the many other things we value, and how all of these assets—or blessings—can be maximized for a life of true abundance and wealth."
—**Whitney Johnson, Thinkers50 Management Thinker and Best-Selling Author of *Build an A Team* and *Disrupt Yourself***

"*The Wealth Creator's Playbook* will help you maximize your return on life and invest in what really matters: dreaming bigger than you thought was possible!"
—**Bob Goff, Founder of Love Does and *New York Times* Best-Selling Author of *Love Does* and *Everybody Always***

"Because we're all human, money can complicate our relationships, consume our focus and even derail our happiness. John is on a mission to help wealth creators ask and answer the question, 'What's my life for?' The answers in this guide, a money book with tremendous heart, will help you maximize your wealth and your life."
—**Howard Behar, Former President, Starbucks Coffee Company North America and Starbucks Coffee International, and Author of *It's Not About the Coffee* and *The Magic Cup***

"*The Wealth Creator's Playbook* offers a unique mix of sound advice for those at various stages of wealth creation and guidance on how to examine the meaning and effects of money on every aspect of your life. For people confronting the wealth bubble and overwhelmed with the task of managing it all, John offers a candid, pragmatic approach to maximizing wealth and fulfillment. The book is a valuable and insightful resource for executives, entrepreneurs, and their families."
—**David Zapolsky, General Counsel, Senior Vice President, and Secretary at Amazon.com**

"*The Wealth Creator's Playbook* offers a unique vision of true wealth: a life of passion, purpose and understanding the meaning behind your money. If you've ever wondered, 'What's the money for?' look no further. I've known John for over ten years, and he is the ultimate guide to aligning your values with your wealth and expanding your vision of what's possible, with the end-goal of maximizing your impact on the world."

—Paul Shoemaker, Founding President, Social Venture Partners International and Author of *Can't Not Do*

"John's approach to wealth through the unique lens of deeply held values and discovering your highest calling encourages wealth creators to construct a life that really means something, putting your money where your heart is."

—Ida Cole, Former Microsoft Vice President, Founder of Seattle Theatre Group

"*The Wealth Creator's Playbook* is a significant resource for anyone experiencing the emotional and practical bumps in the road that come with building a company and wealth. We embrace John's vision of a "life fully lived," using the power of wealth to impact others for good. The tools offered in this book will inspire you to find greater purpose in your own success."

—Scott & Ally Svenson, Founders of MOD Pizza

"John's expertise in wealth management, combined with his role as a life coach, make him uniquely qualified to offer both practical money advice and deeply personal prescriptions for a more healthy and fulfilling life. This book will inspire you to think deeply about your definition of success, how money affects your relationships, and how to align your money and your values. *The Wealth Creator's Playbook* has opened my eyes to the relational and spiritual implications of wealth and inspired me to maximize my resources to live fully and pursue a higher purpose."

—Charles Meyers, CEO of Equinix, Inc.

"What does real success look like? Are my relationships healthy? Am I maximizing my resources to achieve a truly fulfilling life? *The Wealth Creator's Playbook* is for anyone who wants to hit the pause button and examine these vital questions. John offers a practical and spiritual guide to understanding the role money plays in your decisions and relationships, how to align your money with deeply held values, and how wealth can open the door to finding a higher calling and purpose in life."

—Fred Smith, President, The Gathering

The Wealth Creator's Playbook

The Wealth Creator's Playbook

A Guide to Maximizing Your Return on Life and Money

John Christianson

 PRAEGER™

An Imprint of ABC-CLIO, LLC

Santa Barbara, California • Denver, Colorado

Library of Congress Cataloging-in-Publication Data

Names: Christianson, John C., author.
Title: The wealth creator's playbook : a guide to maximizing your return on life and money / John Christianson.
Description: Santa Barbara, CA : Praeger, [2019] | Includes bibliographical references and index.
Identifiers: LCCN 2018051923 (print) | LCCN 2018055199 (ebook) | ISBN 9781440867873 (ebook) | ISBN 9781440867866 (hardback : alk. paper)
Subjects: LCSH: Money—Psychological aspects. | Wealth. | Success. | Finance, Personal.
Classification: LCC HG222.3 (ebook) | LCC HG222.3 .C47 2019 (print) | DDC 332.024/01—dc23
LC record available at https://lccn.loc.gov/2018051923

ISBN: 978-1-4408-6786-6 (print)
        978-1-4408-6787-3 (ebook)

23 22 21 20 19   2 3 4 5

This book is also available as an eBook.

Praeger
An Imprint of ABC-CLIO, LLC

ABC-CLIO, LLC
147 Castilian Drive
Santa Barbara, California 93117
www.abc-clio.com

This book is printed on acid-free paper ∞

Manufactured in the United States of America

To Kelle, my loving and gifted co-creator of our truly wealthy life.

Contents

Acknowledgments

It turns out that wealth creation and writing a book, like other notable markers in life, are best experienced in the company of other people. Not long ago, I was a neophyte author with an idea, and I've been fortunate to be blessed by an incredible team of supporters, teachers, truth-tellers, and experts who all wanted to be part of this journey. Honestly, I really couldn't and wouldn't want to go it alone, anyway. Cheers to all those who contributed to making this book a reality!

Most important, I'm deeply grateful for my wife, Kelle, who has been my partner, co-creator, and chief encourager in business and life. Over three-plus decades, you have always believed in me and what I wanted to accomplish, gave me the space to grow and evolve, and challenged and inspired me to be the best version of myself. Thank you for the encouragement to keep moving forward and the gentle reminders that God has a plan. I love you!

Thank you to my parents, adult kids (and spouses), and my extended family for your unconditional love and support. Specifically, Sherry, Ray, Janet, Mike, and Jeanne, I hope this book honors you and the important influence you've had on my life and whom I've become. In addition, thank you to Colten, Ivy, Trevor, Brooke, Cassius, Danielle, and Ryan. I love you all very much, and you are the essence of true wealth to me.

Thank you to the clients of Highland Private Wealth Management. You allow me into your financial and personal lives, the good and the messy. You gave me the opportunity to develop my skill as a wealth counselor and coach, to hone my theories and business acumen, and to guide and steward your most valued treasures. Without the experience I've gained serving you, I wouldn't be where I am. Thank you for the loyalty, trust, and confidence you placed in me.

Amy Jameson, thank you isn't nearly enough tribute for your editorial and strategic gifts that shaped this book. You taught me how to get my thoughts onto paper, to "skate across the pond" by writing without stopping to judge, dig even further into my soul, and you orchestrated the immense amount of information, concepts, and notes that ultimately formed this book. You are amazing and your editorial touch, strong and candid opinions, keen eye, and motherly encouragement made this book sing.

Thank you to my agent, Joelle Delbourgo, who took a chance on a first-time author and believed that this book needed to be written. Your wise counsel gently encouraged me to be more vulnerable with my story than I believed was possible. Your tenured experience and fierce commitment to this project was invaluable.

Thank you to Hilary Claggett, and the rest of the Praeger publishing team, for getting this book into people's hands. A big thank you to Jessica Fox for always being in my camp and patiently nudging me in the direction of my dreams, Brandon Jameson for the cover design and graphical elements, Anna McClain for the expert research support and strategic thinking, and Kevin, Steven, Susanna, Ian, and Lorrie for the valuable manuscript review and commentary. I also have immense gratitude for the broad list of friends and supporters from church to the rowing club who've encouraged and prayed for me all the way.

Thank you to the fabulous Highland team: Ben J., Ben W., Michael, Colleen, Jeff, Jessica, Nemanja, Cassandra, Michelle, Rick, Dave, and Ed. You cared for our clients and the business while I was chasing this dream. Your lasting contribution is deeply woven into the fabric of my entrepreneurial journey of building an enduring and unique company.

Thank you to *Harvard Business Review* for allowing me to adapt an article I wrote for the magazine entitled, "How to Talk to Your Kids about Money," which was published in the September 2016 issue. This material appears in Chapter Six.

Finally, I want to thank God for the gift of a truly wealthy life: not perfect, but full of incredible blessings, opportunities, meaning, and purpose. I've responded to a calling placed in my heart, and my prayer now is that this book will be an instrument to help wealth creators take hold of the life that is truly life.

Introduction

If you're reading this book, there's a good chance you are a wealth creator or an aspiring wealth creator—a passionate, intelligent, highly motivated, and creative person looking to reap material financial rewards for your hard work. You may just be starting out in a high-potential career, or preparing for such a career, anticipating great rewards to come. Perhaps you have already created considerable wealth and are enjoying the freedom, comforts, and expanded choices that the gift of wealth delivers. Or you may be a future wealth beneficiary, whether through inheritance or a sudden wealth event, like an initial public offering (IPO) or business sale. You also might be a spouse or partner of a wealth creator, experiencing a co-creator role, where your choices, emotional health, and relationships are greatly affected by the wealth flowing into your life. This book is also written with you in mind.

No matter where you are on your journey to wealth, or your role in creating or supporting the creation of wealth, your goal is to be successful: as an individual, as a couple, as a family; in your professional and your personal life. I have the pleasure of working with wealth creators every day. They are smart, talented, and driven to succeed. Through hard work and some lucky breaks, they have amassed significant wealth, and all the benefits that come with it.

What often comes as a surprise to wealth creators is that money comes with its own challenges. Through twenty-five years of advising some of the wealthiest people in the United States on both money and personal matters, I've come to a deep understanding that money is never simple, and success is about so much more than just money.

Wealth creators are no different than anyone else: They want to experience more happiness and fulfillment in their lives, but sometimes the intense pursuit of success can lead to a widening gap between your ideal life and the one you are currently experiencing. You may feel stuck, wishing for a different definition of success. Money may become an issue in your relationships. You may find yourself wondering, "What's the money for?"

In cultures around the world, money is often seen as the de facto score-card for success. Or, as venture capitalist Joel Solomon quips: "Capitalism is perhaps the dominant religion in the world today." Many have embraced this religion of wealth wholeheartedly. According to the *Global Wealth Report 2017,* issued by Credit Suisse Research Institute, "The number of millionaires in the world has increased by 155 percent and the number of ultra high net worth individuals (defined as people with a net worth above US $50 million) increased by 216 percent since 2000. 51 percent of these ultra high net worth individuals reside in North America."[1]

The *Global Wealth Report* forecasts that the United States will have the highest growth in the number of millionaires in the world over the next five years.[2] We are also living through an unprecedented time, when an estimated $50 trillion of assets will be transferred and/or inherited by 2061, representing the largest transfer of wealth in history. Beginning in 2031, 10 percent of all wealth in the United States will change hands every five years. More and more individuals are going to experience both the bene-fits and the challenges of wealth.

Because it is such a loaded and often taboo subject, we carry around a lot of psychological baggage regarding our relationship to money. And when we experience a change in our financial situation, particularly com-ing into a large amount of money, we may find that everything we believed about ourselves, our relationships, and our place in the world has shifted.

There is a saying that goes, "Money can't fix a problem it didn't create," and so more of it won't help either. In other words, money isn't the secret elixir that will solve your self-confidence problems, cure the wounds from your family, improve your marriage, make you a better parent, or even make you happy. In my experience, money will serve to amplify what is already present in your life—for better or worse. Much like putting gaso-line on a fire, it will ignite the combustible material present at the time.

High material wealth can actually be associated with low psychological well-being. In a special issue of *American Psychologist* focusing on the mental-health aspects of wealth, David M. Buss, a professor of psychology at the University of Texas at Austin, noted that rates of depression are higher in more economically developed countries than in less developed coun-tries.[3] According to psychologist David G. Myers, when compared to their counterparts in the 1950s, "[Americans] are twice as rich and no happier.

Meanwhile, the divorce rate doubled. Teen suicide tripled. . . . Depression rates have soared, especially among teens and young adults. . . . I call this conjunction of material prosperity and social recession *the American paradox*. The more people strive for extrinsic goals such as money, the more numerous their problems and the less robust their well being."[4]

Noted for his work in the study of happiness and creativity, Hungarian psychologist Mihaly Csikszentmihalyi has reasoned that "to the extent that most of one's psychic energy becomes invested in material goals, it is typical for sensitivity to other rewards to atrophy. Friendships, art, literature, natural beauty, religion, and philosophy become less and less interesting."[5] Wealth may bring material comfort and certain freedoms, but it often comes at a steep psychological cost.

Wealth can also be a fickle mistress. According to Ric Edelman, writing in *Fortune*, "the Certified Financial Planner Board of Standards says nearly a third of lottery winners declare bankruptcy—meaning they were worse off than before they became rich. Other studies show that lottery winners frequently become estranged from family and friends, and incur a greater incidence of depression, drug and alcohol abuse, divorce, and suicide than the average American."[6]

There is an old proverb, "Shirtsleeves to shirtsleeves in three generations," referring to a common scenario where wealth created by the first generation is squandered and spent by the time the third generation passes. The first generation creates the wealth through passion, persistence, and hard work. The second generation sees these values but is often protected from experiencing the grit it took to create the wealth in the first place, as they enjoy a greatly improved lifestyle they didn't earn themselves. By the third generation, maintaining the lifestyle becomes the norm, and the family values are a distant memory.

As wealth becomes an expectation rather than an aspiration, the relative enjoyment of the benefits provided by wealth tends to decrease. Just as in a situation of addiction, once individuals have strived for and attained a certain level of wealth, it becomes the norm and ceases to be fulfilling. Achieving the next level up can become all-consuming.[7] Csikszentmihalyi notes that "wealth, like many good things, is beneficial in small quantities, but it becomes increasingly desired and ultimately can become harmful in large doses."[8]

My experience working with clients who are building wealth has taught me that money often becomes an obstacle in their lives. At the center of the problem are trust and empathy. Successful wealth creators often isolate themselves as a reaction to their inability to find people they can confide in. They come into my office with a bagful of unspoken concerns and lingering questions, needing an outlet to discuss and process their fears. I see the palpable relief they experience simply by being heard, understood, and validated. Confidence builds as they realize they are not alone in their experience, that they have a partner and guide to show them the way forward.

The addition of wealth creates new opportunities and new challenges. You may not have to worry about paying the bills as much, or even talk about money as often, but if you lacked passion at your job before the money arrived, wealth will not cure that ailment. You may have much more time on your hands and a broader spectrum of choices due to your sudden increase in wealth. It can feel like anything is possible, which is a wonderful gift, but having too many options can be a burden for some. Freedom from having to work sounds wonderful in theory, but often boredom sets in, and a lack of purpose and identity results from not having anything meaningful to do. The fact is, wealth creators and aspiring wealth creators are largely unprepared, both emotionally and practically, for how wealth will affect their lives.

I wrote *The Wealth Creator's Playbook* to help you navigate the rough psychological waters that wealth creators often swim in. Throughout the book, we'll reconsider the definition of "success"; explore your money emotional intelligence; identify common emotional roadblocks around money, such as family and marital relationships, kids and money, and generosity and identity; investigate how your values align with your money; and explore insights into and opportunities around your highest contribution or calling. Through intentional processes, including diagnostic assessment tools and personal stories from clients, wealth creators can emerge from being stressed and stuck when it comes to money, to find hope, peace of mind, and real happiness. (Note: All names have been changed and certain details have been modified or generalized to protect the privacy of the individuals involved.)

A playbook is a set of strategies—a framework to help you think through your options, take action, and achieve a goal. This playbook will help you formulate a personalized plan applicable to your unique life and money circumstances. Certain chapters may be more relevant to your current needs, while others may simply be good information to have for the future, as your wealth grows and its impacts on your life change. My recommendation would be to read the book in its entirety to get a complete understanding of the issues and opportunities affecting wealth creators of all stripes.

I believe wholeheartedly that wealth is a gift. Calling it a "gift" may seem to devalue the years of intense effort and focused talent needed to create wealth. Wealth creation is labor-intensive and involves many sacrifices. Nonetheless, when you look at statistics around wealth and poverty worldwide, you can only feel blessed and lucky to have the undergirding of health, family, education, opportunity, and infrastructure that makes wealth creation possible.

I define wealth as more than just money: Wealth also includes my life, health, and relationships. All these are gifts—or spiritually speaking, blessings—I've been given by God to both enjoy and to steward wisely. When we look at wealth as a gift, we start to turn our thinking from managing the gift to maximizing it.

Wealth creators are regularly offered practical solutions to help them manage the gift, and there are many other books and resources available about creating and protecting wealth. *Managing* the gift of wealth and *maximizing* it are very different concepts. Managing the gift of wealth includes things like stock option exercise planning, asset allocation strategies, tax-efficient investment, college education savings alternatives, and insurance coverage reviews—which are all valuable, practical actions to take. However, you won't find advice about managing the gift of wealth in this book; this is not your typical "how to get rich" investment guide.

While *The Wealth Creator's Playbook* provides advice on the practical implications of money, the aim of this book is to help you consider higher purposes for the gift of wealth—in other words, *maximizing* the gift of wealth. At the end of your life, you will look back and evaluate whether you used this gift to pursue your passions, do the things you love, and to impact your world in positive ways. These are the metrics you will use to measure your ultimate "success."

I'm on a mission to change your relationship with and perspective about money, and help answer the question: "What's the money for?" My hope is that you will no longer see money as something to control and obsess over. Neither will it be an end in itself, as if having a rich, full life were completely dependent on money. I want you to win at the game of money and life. Wealth creators have a huge advantage that most people don't have. We'll unlock the hidden potential and opportunity for contribution that money presents.

The simple truth is, I want your life to flourish because of *who you are,* not because of your wealth. You aren't your money, but how you spend, invest, maximize, and relate to it speaks volumes about who you are and what you care about. Enjoying a healthy relationship with wealth ultimately depends on understanding who you are, why you exist, and where your unique contribution lies. I'll show you how to focus your energies and your wealth outward, to flourish and become fulfilled. I want you to have it all: a truly rich life.

Let's jump in!

CHAPTER ONE

Redefining Success

It was 1985, and I was an out-of-work certified public accountant (CPA) who had recently been laid off by a global accounting firm in Seattle after only two years on the job. With my pride bruised, and feeling like a failure, I decided to sign up for the stockbroker trainee program with Dean Witter Reynolds & Co. Several friends were making a good living as brokers, and the stock market was starting to reach new highs. The stockbroker role seemed like a better fit for my relationship skills and abilities than being an accountant, and I really wanted a job where I could help people.

Over five grit-tested years, I built a brokerage clientele through what was referred to as "smiling and dialing," the popular method for reaching prospects during that decade. My goal each day was to cold-call a minimum of 40–60 residences or businesses in my local area with an investment idea and open new accounts that would lead to future investment sales and commissions. After the 12-month training period ended, my pay was 100 percent commissions-based, and that was all the incentive I needed to learn quickly how to become proficient at selling stocks, bonds, and mutual funds to anyone who would listen to me.

The grind of commission sales became more and more of a challenge partly because of my original CPA training as a trusted resource, and also my desire to be viewed by clients as something other than just a salesman. Fortunately, as my tolerance for cold-calling was running low, I was approached by my wife's uncle, who was working for a wealthy family in San Diego that recently experienced a major liquidity event from an initial public offering (IPO). They were setting up a family office in Bellevue, Washington, and needed to fill a chief financial officer (CFO) role. Their ideal candidate needed experience in the financial markets and would work directly with the family patriarch and chief executive officer (CEO). I jumped at the chance to shift my career focus closer to what I believed was calling me forward in my personal evolution.

The traditional family office was the genesis of the wealth management industry we have today. For many years, multigenerational wealthy families created central financial hubs where all financial matters for the family were handled, including investing, accounting, property management, estate planning, and legal, insurance, and other financial and concierge-type functions, such as travel. The goal of this unified approach is to protect and maintain the privacy of family assets through professional management, coordinated results, improved efficiency and costs, and streamlined communications through the family office.

My CFO role in this family office exposed me to a world I had never experienced before: family assets of over $100 million (in 1990), commercial real estate development and leasing activities; a significant stock portfolio; several operating companies; extravagant personal residences, cars, and airplanes; a world-class investment and legal team; and about ten office employees. I was starting to understand what it felt like to have a seat at the table as a trusted advisor, with access to comprehensive and confidential details about finances and family objectives, as well as the ability to influence decisions.

It didn't take me long to become curious about who else performed this type of holistic and conflict-free advisory service to wealth creators. Microsoft was just starting to mint new millionaires, and I was confident that there would be a demand for the comprehensive wealth management services I experienced in the family office setting. This next generation of wealth creators wanted an approach that would provide most of the benefits of a full-blown family office, with much lower cost and hassle factors.

I saw a clear vision of where the financial advisor business was heading, and my quest to engage in this line of work led me to a very unique company doing multiclient advisory work based in Silicon Valley. They understood the needs of these new wealth creators and were building a platform to serve them. They recognized the growing technology field and the new wealth being created in the Pacific Northwest, and I opened their first satellite office in Seattle.

It seemed like I had it all: I had obtained advanced designations (CPA and CFA) and an engaging career, and I was happily married, with three young kids attending excellent private schools, a new house in the suburbs, and a dog. I regularly attended church and participated in several nonprofit activities, and I was making more money than ever before, working with clients at cool technology companies. I was checking all the "success" boxes in terms of life and money.

However, under the surface, something wasn't right. I was experiencing anxiety symptoms that were becoming more and more frequent and pronounced. At one meeting with a major estate-planning group in Seattle, I was visibly sweating and uncomfortable and had a difficult time speaking. I was also increasingly at odds with the direction of the company I worked for and the life philosophy of the owners. It can be difficult to be in the satellite office of a firm: You are outside the culture and don't rub shoulders day to day with key players, including your bosses. The upside was I had tremendous freedom to build client relationships and set up the office the way I wanted to.

The owners wanted to see my satellite office grow even faster, and they decided to expand the leadership team beyond me to protect client relationships should I decide to leave. Several new employees were added to the office, including the nephew of one of the owners. We were intentionally put into direct competition with each other; there was friction about prospects and referral sources, and virtually no trust. From my perspective, the owners were focused on getting rich at all costs, prioritizing work and status over relationships and suggesting that life balance was for the weak. Money, and lots of it, was their sole aim, regardless of consequences. I was just beginning to understand that my own purpose and career objectives were grounded at a much deeper level.

In January 1999, I made a routine trip to Menlo Park, California, to the company headquarters. The office was on Sand Hill Road, a prestigious address in the epicenter of new-tech money south of San Francisco. The event was my annual performance review, given by the two owners of the firm. I was performing well enough on paper, but my body was telling a different story.

Perry, one of the owners, suggested to me during my review that I was duplicitous. (At the time, I didn't know what that word meant and had to go look it up.) Perry recognized an incongruence between the "Everything is great" story I was telling and the underlying emotions I was experiencing and not sharing. The world of success and big money had collided with my life view, and they weren't in harmony.

Perry's comment really shook me because I lived by the virtue of honesty, and in that moment, I realized I wasn't being honest with the owners or myself. I wasn't intentionally being deceptive, but there was an internal wrestling match going on around my lack of happiness and fulfillment and my evolving definition of success. Perry gave me a gift that day by telling me the truth of what he saw.

Does Money Equal Success?

By all outward measures, I had achieved "success" at this point in my life. But I wasn't happy, healthy, or at peace. Unfortunately, this is true for many "successful" wealth creators. I worked with a fortysomething venture capitalist named Rob who had achieved a substantial amount of wealth early in his career. He admitted that creating the wealth took a big toll on his life—it required maniacal focus and all his energy, resulted in broken relationships, and required him to put his own wellness on the back burner.

I asked him: Would he change anything if he could go back in time? His response seemed contrary to common sense: He said he would likely do it the same way again because he wanted to have the financial resources to choose his life, send his kids to private school, and enjoy other lifestyle comforts. I share this story because I believe it represents a formula that many of us follow simply because it's the only one we know. Work ridiculously hard, create success in the form of wealth and power, and sacrifice our health and relationships along the way, in the hope of someday figuring out the life we really want, when we have time to think about it.

In an interview, best-selling author and vulnerability expert Brené Brown advised: "Defining success is one of the most powerful things you can do as a family, as a couple, individually. There is a default definition [of success] that is, 'money, materialism, accomplishment, and achievement.'" Brown explains that burnout and damage to our physical and mental health are often the result when we narrowly focus on achieving traditional measures of success (namely, money and power).[9]

Obviously, money is a powerful motivator, and as my client Rob expressed, he was willing to sacrifice his time, energy, health, and relationships for the comforts, choices, and "freedom" that money provided. It seems a very normal path for many to empire-build earlier in life. In my own life, I've seen evidence of this pattern, especially in my 30s. Our culture promotes the idea of success being defined by material possessions: houses, cars, "stuff"—everything money can buy. All this stuff is supposed to make us happy. A 2010 study from Princeton University demonstrates that once someone achieves an annual salary of $75,000, they don't report any greater degree of day-to-day happiness, no matter how much their income increases.[10] Once our basic needs are met, the utility of money as a component of satisfaction starts to level off.

There is another, deeper reason Rob stayed focused on financial outcomes exclusively: because it keeps us distracted from having to author our life—something we aren't taught how to do. If we stay distracted with empire building and financial security, we don't have to dig into the uncertain world of knowing ourselves and defining and designing a future. It's just easier to try to win on our financial scorecard. And to be fair, the busyness of demanding professions combined with raising a family and keeping up with many responsibilities leave many wealth creators with little time to consider the impacts and outcomes of success and money in their lives.

A Richer Definition of Success

There is nothing wrong with wanting it all. I wanted more for my life back in 1999, when I realized I couldn't continue on my current path. I wanted to flourish in every facet of my life—financial, career satisfaction, family, health, and other personal goals that mattered to me—and I wanted adventure to go along with it. I only had one life to live, and I wanted more passion and purpose. I wanted to know myself better and heal from the anxiety that plagued me. I wanted to go on a spiritual journey that required putting my faith into action. I wanted to understand what I was made of, what made me tick, and what was possible.

I wanted the time to coach my son's baseball team and to be an active and available parent for our kids. I wanted to spend more quality time with my wife. I wanted to put my stamp on the world by creating and innovating a business culture that valued caring for people, pursuing excellence, personal growth and development, and life fully lived. I also wanted to build wealth, experience financial success and security, and be generous.

Starting a company was a long shot when I was younger, but at age 37, I felt this was my last chance to create the future I desperately wanted. There was a lot at stake: We had become financially comfortable with my salary and its accompanying lifestyle perks. We had ratcheted up our spending commensurate with my raises, and I definitely didn't want my lifestyle to backslide. Regardless, it was clear to me that in a few short years I'd be 50, and I didn't want to be financially comfortable, unhappy, full of regrets, and stuck.

During the next three months, I began preparing to launch my own business—I secured a small executive office space, bought a computer, picked a company name, made a list of projects and priorities, and prayed a lot. There were many long talks with my wife, Kelle, about what I planned to do. She was my life partner and the co-creator of our wealth, and I knew I wouldn't be able to move forward without her support, trust, and commitment. We needed to be in complete alignment.

On May 5, 1999, the night before the planned launch date, I was full of fear and anxiety because of what I was about to risk. I remember feeling like I was at the top of a very large cliff, looking down at the water below. I was literally scared to death, unable to sleep; the pressure in my chest was overwhelming, not sure if the water below was safe.

The next morning, I jumped. The water was fine, and Highland was born.

In the nineteen years since then, I've lived my way to a richer definition of success. I realized that I didn't want financial success at the cost of missing all the other sweetness of life during the journey. Some components of redefining success for myself included:

- Money does not exclusively equate to success in life.
- You don't need to sacrifice your health, your relationships, and other important life objectives to build wealth.
- Experiences are more valuable than stuff.
- Generosity is the secret joy creator.
- Understand where the boundary is between "enough" and "more than enough."
- Consciously set the level of your lifestyle and resist it creeping higher.
- Strive for continuous learning and growth.
- Achieve alignment with your spouse around shared values.
- Know what the money is for. — *But you can plan it ahead.*

I believe we will end up with a better life outcome if we take a more holistic and thoughtful approach to defining success, moving beyond purely financial objectives. You can't take the money with you when you die, and as many studies have shown, it doesn't increase happiness.

In a 2018 interview, the comedian and actor Jim Carrey talked about "getting to the place where you have everything everybody has ever desired and realizing you are still unhappy."[11] Journalist and author Kirsten Powers points out in an article in *USA Today* that we live in a culture of disconnection from family, friends, and our communities, while relentlessly pursuing the outward trappings of success: a promotion, a raise, a new car or house. She writes: "We are too busy trying to 'make it' without realizing that once we reach that goal, it won't be enough. . . . In many ways achieving all your goals provides the opposite of fulfillment: It lays bare the truth that there is nothing you can purchase, possess, or achieve that will make you feel fulfilled over the long term."[12]

What if our definition of success shifted to "significance" instead? What choices would we make if we believed that our lives matter much more than our pocketbooks—that success is measured by the kind of person you become, the quality and depth of your relationships, the empathy you show, the generosity you share with those in need?

The millennial generation is embracing a new way to look at life that is broader and more robust. They are breaking down the idea that money is the end-all, and the only objective measure of success. They don't want to waste their prime years focused exclusively on empire building. They want to taste the fruit along the way, not just near the end of the journey when success is assured. While the American Dream is built on acquiring material goods, millennials would rather collect experiences than things.

According to a survey conducted by Harris and sponsored by the Web platform Eventbrite, "[T]his generation not only highly values experiences, but they are increasingly spending time and money on them: from concerts and social events to athletic pursuits, to cultural experiences and events of all kinds. For this group, happiness isn't as focused on possessions or career status. Living a meaningful, happy life is about creating, sharing, and capturing memories earned through experiences that span the spectrum of life's opportunities."[13]

Millennials also expect more from their jobs. According to the 2015 Deloitte Millennial Survey, which researched more than 7,700 millennials spanning 29 countries, 6 out of 10 respondents said that "a sense of purpose" is why they chose to work for their current employer.[14] Millennials also aren't chasing jobs for higher salaries—they are looking for companies that share their personal values. According to the same survey, 7 out of 10 believe that the company they work for shares the same personal values as them.

The joy really is in the journey. This is why experiences enrich our lives more than stuff. Alice, a *Fortune* 100 executive, found "significance" in designing life experiences for her family. Recently, she took her son to Japan on a mother-son spring break adventure. Although she could afford to book five-star hotels and travel first class, Alice specifically chose coach airline tickets and staying at an Airbnb.

She wants her kids to stay grounded, experience what scarcity looks like, and understand that you can have great experiences without spending a lot of money. Her goal was to build a wealth of family experiences that would be remembered and valued. Isn't it interesting that what we really treasure is our memories with people we love and care for? Those satisfy, whereas more stuff is just an endless game of "bigger and better" that never really ends.

Maximizing Your Life

Redefining what success looks like for you is the first step toward maximizing your return on life. When money is the only metric we measure, we can easily become obsessed with hitting a certain financial target rather than finding satisfaction in our relationships, experiences, and other goals. Each of us needs to find our level of financial "enoughness."

This can be challenging for driven wealth creators, who often live in the financially skewed bubbles of high-income, high-growth communities, such as Silicon Valley, New York City, Seattle, and elsewhere. It's easy to feel relatively middle class in places where there is always someone with greater assets, a bigger house, a nicer car, and even an airplane, where everything is expensive (especially real estate and education) and neighbors are enjoying an everyday lavish lifestyle. You quickly become used to a certain level of spending, and lifestyle creep is difficult to control. "Enough" is never quite enough when we compare our wealth to those with more than us. If you never put a boundary around your needs, the line keeps moving, and financial security will always be just beyond your reach.

Christopher, the CEO of a successful start-up in Seattle, shared with me that his goal was to reach $10 million of liquid assets, in addition to his valuable home and vacation properties. He told me this was his "F-you money." I asked him to define what he meant by that and why it was so important to him. He told me this was the "minimum" amount of money where he could literally do whatever he wanted and didn't have to play "the game" anymore. By hitting this number in his bank account, he felt he would be immune from needing a job or to rely on anyone else.

This extreme desire to separate ourselves and be self-sufficient is unhealthy and creates unnatural hoarding and accumulation drives. The need for financial security is grounded in our desire to control the uncertainty of the world around us. But we falsely believe that if we have a large-enough asset base, we can mute our volatile emotions and find peace in the "safety" of amassing the biggest pile.

I encourage you to sit down and calculate what financial "enoughness" looks like for you. Either through a wealth advisor or using any number of free online tools and resources (see the Appendix for more details), you can create a financial plan that evaluates the sustainability of your current rate of expenses, relative to your income and savings, in order to determine the probability of having enough to meet your planned needs. Estimates on certain expenses and expectations are important to try to pin down, such as inflation, taxes, and investment returns, because they play an outsized role in the results. Also, keep in mind that certain expenses are affected by inflation more than others, such as college tuition and medical costs.

It's best to consider this exercise as part reality and part envisioning your desired future—a way to gain a more realistic picture of the asset base you will need to fund your hopes and dreams. The beauty of most financial planning software tools is that you can make adjustments based on various assumptions, changing the variables to immediately see how differences in income and expenses affect the end result. This exercise is a useful tool in strategically designing your financial life to include your needs, wants, and wishes. Seeing actual numbers helps build confidence and clarity.

Of course, life can change quickly, and so can financial assumptions, but by revisiting these calculations at least annually, you can review your commitment to your outcomes and see what adjustments need to be made. It can also be an opportunity to draw a circle around your lifestyle spending and look for opportunities to improve your stewardship of the resources you have, preserving the excess, and building a "more than enough" pot for contributions to people and causes you care about.

When we step back and take a good hard look, the level of abundance of any wealth creator when compared to the rest of the world is staggering, where the top 1 percent income level globally is about $45,000. That puts wealth creators, and much of the middle class, in the stratosphere of wealth compared to their global brethren, with no need to worry about obtaining basic necessities and plenty of opportunity to acquire anything on their list of desires.

Ironically, studies on generosity conducted by Christian Smith and Hilary Davidson at Notre Dame University demonstrate that by clinging to what we have and protecting ourselves against future uncertainties and misfortunes, we become more anxious and are actually more vulnerable to future misfortunes. Generosity is the secret joy creator. When we focus on making a significant difference in the lives of others, we enhance our own well-being. Smith and Davidson's research shows a consistent link between demonstrating generosity and leading a better life: Generous people are happier, suffer fewer illnesses and injuries, live with a greater sense of purpose, and experience less depression.[15]

One of the benefits of calculating your level of financial independence is gaining clarity about your gifting capacity—the resources you have over and above your needs, which you could give away, now or in the future. (We will review gifting capacity and philanthropy more in depth in Chapter Three.) I believe that many people aren't more generous because they really don't know what they can afford to give, so they sit on their hands.

Knowing that you can give, and how much, is empowering. This is the quantitative aspect of giving: crunching the numbers to determine your financial ability to give. The next element is qualitative in nature, derived from your personal definition of generosity. Kelle and I approach generosity from a faith perspective that suggests contributing 10 percent of our income to church and other charities. We haven't always reached that level of giving in the past, but our commitments are leading us in that direction.

The final element is experiential, where your heart is drawn to give through personal experience. This is where aspiring wealth creators can experiment with giving, even small amounts like $50 or $100 to charities that interest them, and begin creating an emotional connection to one or more charities or causes. The amount of money is secondary to connecting your heart to what ultimately drives a very personal decision about how much to give.

Once you have a clear picture of how much money you need to achieve your life vision, you can determine how to define "enoughness" for yourself. Additional wealth becomes surplus, and this is where the heavy lifting starts. This is where we can begin figuring out for ourselves what that money is for. Because I only have one life to live, I want my life to be the best it possibly can be, and not just financially. Life, just like wealth, is a gift, and we all desire a meaningful return on investment. What a shame it would be to live a small, minimized, underproductive, and ineffective life. When I look back, I want to have maximized my life and to have lived it to the fullest.

I want all wealth creators to experience the richness of life I've been blessed to enjoy through discovering a new definition of success. In refocusing my life on relating, creating, learning, and giving, I've found this to be true: Success is about so much more than money.

In the next chapters, we'll explore the practical realities and emotional undercurrents for wealth creators as they journey through the Wealth Life Cycle and learn to manage the complexity that comes with increasing wealth.

QUESTIONS TO CONSIDER AS YOU EXPLORE YOUR OWN RELATIONSHIP WITH MONEY AND SUCCESS:

- What is your current definition of success?
- What do you worry about related to your financial life?
- How much is "enough" for you?

CHAPTER TWO

New Millionaires and the Wealth Life Cycle

Wealth creation has become a way of life in the world today. A record number of Americans are joining the millionaire's club. As of 2017, there were 15.3 million people worth $1 million or more in the United States, and 36 million millionaires worldwide. In fact, three thousand new millionaires were minted every day in the United States in 2016–2017[16]—that's more than two millionaires every minute.

Who are these new wealth creators? (Note that wherever the term "wealth creator" is used, I'm referring not only to those who have already secured material wealth, but also aspiring wealth creators, who strive to achieve wealth in the future.)

Wealth creators generally don't come from a life of privilege. They are usually the first generation in their families to have achieved wealth. Their parents may not have been poor, and many describe their upbringing as middle class and sometimes upper middle class, but just as often, they were raised in a house just outside the boundary of a nice neighborhood.

Their parents didn't achieve significant wealth, even though they may have been successful in their own right as teachers, professionals, or tradespeople. Many wealth creators had to work hard to get what they wanted in life, from a young age, and had the drive to make something of themselves. They are usually highly educated and driven to do very interesting, stimulating, or "cool" work with others like themselves. Achieving wealth isn't always their career aim, but money is definitely a motivator.

Wealth creators are "new money," as opposed to "old money." Old money is multigenerational, has the trappings of family offices, history, and patriarchal and matriarchal figures who provide financial leadership to younger generations. New money is first-generational, without clear role models or experience with rising wealth levels, and its members have a grounding in frugality from their past.

Wealth creators may have received wealth that's disproportionate to their input into a business or activity, and they know they are lucky. They may be so-called "accidental millionaires." Many who have achieved wealth through entrepreneurship, successful start-ups, or a fortuitous business sale face the reality that they were really lucky to be in the right place at the right time in history.

This was clearly the case at Microsoft, where the specific years of employment had huge, widely varying impacts on individual net worth. For example, employees in the 1990s saw great expansion in stock prices and brokerage accounts, while mediocre stock performance at Microsoft during the 2000s did not produce the same employee payoffs (with the exception of the past three years). For employees paid in stock options or other stock-based compensation, timing truly is everything. Being at, or starting, the right high-growth company is the key to realizing immense financial rewards for a huge investment of mental and emotional energy.

Wealth creators want to work on important and interesting projects, in high-achieving roles. They gravitate to companies where outsized financial rewards are associated with achieving success. Many wealth creators are concentrated in cities where start-up capital is flowing and entrepreneurs thrive, such as Silicon Valley, Seattle, Boston, Atlanta, Austin, and Los Angeles.

They want to work with others who are highly intelligent and who will challenge them, where youth isn't viewed as a liability and innovation is rewarded. They seek fast-paced environments with movement toward a mission and a culture of meritocracy; however, the stress and intensity of their focus on achieving their goals can wreak havoc on their personal lives.

Wealth creators may have experienced a "sudden wealth" event. This category includes those who work at companies that launch an initial public offering (IPO) and all of the options and stock earned became liquid and real overnight. Other sudden wealth events include receiving an inheritance, selling a business, receiving an insurance settlement, or winning the lottery. I include those who experience these other sudden wealth events as wealth creators because the emotional and financial realities they experience are very consistent with other new wealth creators.

Whether they work all their lives to achieve wealth or it happens suddenly through an IPO or an unexpected windfall, wealth creators all have one thing in common: they are new to big money and they have no idea how it will change their lives.

Two Sides of the Wealth Coin

Of course, wealth creators understand and appreciate the upside of wealth. Who wouldn't enjoy the freedom to choose whether or not to work, and having time to spend on projects and causes you care about—not to mention time to spend with the people you love, in places you've dreamed of visiting, enjoying a lifestyle of comfort and even luxury? Wealth truly is a gift.

But wealth also comes with many unrecognized pitfalls and risk factors. Wealth can increase isolation: Wealth creators tend to play alone, work alone, be alone, and have a higher susceptibility to depression and anxiety. Suniya S. Luthar, professor of psychology at Arizona State University, writes: "Wealthy communities can, paradoxically, be among those most likely to engender feelings of friendlessness and isolation in their inhabitants. Physical characteristics of wealthy suburban communities may contribute to feelings of isolation. Houses in these communities are often set far apart with privacy of all ensured by long driveways, high hedges, and sprawling lawns."[17] In other words, the wealthy are physically isolated from interaction with others.

As wealth increases, so does the ability to buy services that have traditionally been taken care of through family, neighbors, or community efforts. Luthar notes, "Affluent individuals are amply able to purchase various services such as psychotherapy for depression, medical care for physical illness, and professional caregivers for children, and in not having to rely on friends for such assistance, they rarely obtain direct 'proof' of others' authentic concern. In essence, therefore, the rich are the least likely to experience the security of deep social connectedness that is routinely enjoyed by people in communities where mutual dependence is often unavoidable."[18]

Affluence leads to a lack of dependent relationships, which can leave the wealthy feeling socially disconnected and lacking a sense of community. Part of this relational isolation stems from the endless choices available to wealth creators: they can choose to be part of any number of churches, clubs, and social groups, and leave them whenever they want. Ironically, too much freedom to choose actually dilutes our sense of belonging and connection to a particular group.

I believe there is a tight correlation between levels of wealth and the isolation that wealth creators experience. Those new to wealth may find that there are fewer and fewer people who can relate to their situation. They may have trouble finding friends who can appreciate what they are wrestling with—both the positive and negative impacts of wealth. They often confront jealousy among old friends and family members, hearing statements like "You're so lucky" from envious onlookers who see lifestyle changes happening.

For those new to wealth, guilt is often a factor, both that they have more than those around them, and that they cannot openly express any negative feelings they may be experiencing around the challenges that come with wealth. Psychotherapists report that affluent individuals commonly struggle with confusion and guilt about their distress. One therapist reported: "I cannot begin to count the number of times that an expensively dressed, immaculately groomed woman drove her luxury car into my parking area, walked gracefully into my office, sat down, and announced, 'My life is perfect. I have everything I could ask for,' and then, bursting into tears, 'Why am I so unhappy? This makes no sense at all—I must get over this!'"[19]

Another risk factor for wealth creators: Several studies show that the higher you rise on the socioeconomic ladder, the less ethical, more selfish, and more self-centered you may become. You only have to look at the news to see a regular stream of celebrities and successful business leaders who act like they are the center of the universe and believe that laws don't apply to them.

In a series of seven studies conducted by social scientist Paul K. Piff and colleagues at the University of California, Berkeley (UC Berkeley), upper-class participants behaved more unethically than lower-class participants, including being more likely to break the law while driving, take valued goods from others, exhibit unethical decision-making, lie in a negotiation, cheat to increase their chances of winning, and endorse unethical behavior at work. "While having money doesn't necessarily make anybody anything," Piff says, "the rich are way more likely to prioritize their own self-interests above the interests of other people. It makes them more likely to exhibit characteristics that we would stereotypically associate with, say, assholes."[20]

Why do upper-class individuals appear to be more prone to these behaviors? The authors of this study suggest: "Upper-class individuals' relative independence from others and increased privacy in their professions may provide fewer structural constraints and decreased perceptions of risk associated with committing unethical acts. The availability of resources to deal with the downstream costs of unethical behavior may increase the likelihood of such acts among the upper class." They also suggest that the self-perception of upper-class individuals may lead them to feel entitled and to disregard the consequences of their actions on others.[21] Again, isolation appears to be a contributing factor to these behaviors.

In many ways, wealth has the potential to change people for the worse: We've already discussed the potential for increased isolation, unethical behavior, selfishness, and depression, but wealth also can reduce impulses toward generosity, empathy, and compassion. In studies conducted at UC Berkeley in 2011, psychologist Jennifer Steller's research demonstrated that students from upper-middle-class and wealthy backgrounds scored much lower on compassionate behaviors than their lower-income classmates.

Students were asked to self-report on compassionate behaviors in one study, and in another, the participants were hooked up to heart-rate monitors while watching a compassion-inducing video. "We have found that, during compassion, the heart rate lowers as if the body is calming itself to take care of another person," Stellar says. The lower-income students experienced a measurable slowing of heart rate, a physiological marker of the experience of compassion, during the video. Stellar notes that higher-income students may have just as much capacity to feel compassion, but they may simply lack experience observing and tending to the hardships of others.[22] Again, the isolating effects of wealth can limit opportunities to experience firsthand what suffering looks like and to know how to respond appropriately.

I regularly review tax returns with millions of dollars in income listed (and with assets even greater), only to see a minimal amount, or sometimes nothing at all, on the line for charitable contributions. For example, someone worth $20 million, with an adjusted gross income (AGI) of $1 million for the year, might have charitable giving of only $25,000. In and of itself, that is a big number, but relative to this person's level of affluence, it is quite small—only a small percentage of overall assets.

I see this tendency often as I consult with those who are new to wealth: Their first impulse is to focus on building more wealth before engaging in any significant philanthropy. In fact, this is true for a majority of higher-income households: As income level rises, a higher percentage of households make charitable contributions, but donations level off at around 2 percent to 3 percent of income. While fewer very-low-income households give anything to charity, those who do donate give an average of 12 percent of their income (for households earning $25,000 or less).[23]

Considering the potential emotional and psychological downsides to attaining wealth, you may be asking yourself: Why would anyone want to become a millionaire? The Bible says that the love of money is the root of all evil. But is wealth really all bad? I don't think there is anything innately wrong with making money and enjoying the fruits of our labor. The evil is in what we have turned money into: from a gift and blessing into a form of control, power, and unhealthy self-sufficiency.

Wealth can be like gravity, pushing us inward and insulating us from life, driving us to achieve a sick version of independence where we don't need anyone or anything. We believe we are in charge and the ultimate arbitrator of what happens: a god of sorts. Many embrace the false belief that storing up a larger and larger pile of resources will protect us from difficulties and pain in life, or that joy can come only through the continual acquisition of more. What is clear from research and my own experience is that those who drive into palatial homes each night, protected in their castles of the twenty-first century, feel the same pangs of loneliness and desire for greater connection, fulfillment, and purpose as everyone else on the other side of the moat.

The Wealth Life Cycle

Having the tools to embrace the benefits of wealth and dodge the pitfalls begins with an understanding of what I call the "Wealth Life Cycle." The practical ramifications of wealth don't develop at the same time as the emotional impacts, and both categories can be greatly influenced by which stage of wealth creation you are experiencing. After many years of working with successful wealth creators, I have seen certain patterns emerge as their level of wealth increases and time elapses. The Wealth Life Cycle generally moves through three phases: Creating, Managing, and Relating.

Phase 1 of the Wealth Life Cycle is the "Creating Wealth" stage, and the goal is amassing enough money to buy time freedom and expanded choices. Often, the end goal is the ability to retire (or at least stop working at your current job) and focus on other projects and passions. In this phase, wealth creators want to feel financially safe—knowing that they will have enough money to sustain their lifestyle and pay the bills when they are no longer working for a living. In Phase 1, you may be asking yourself:

- What's my number?
- Is this enough to create the future lifestyle I want?
- What is the best way to get liquid, and when can this happen?
- Do I need a financial advisor?

You begin to experience some of the emotional stresses around wealth during this phase, such as worrying about how much is enough and how wealth will affect your career trajectory and sense of purpose associated with your work life. You also may experience regret, confusion, and even

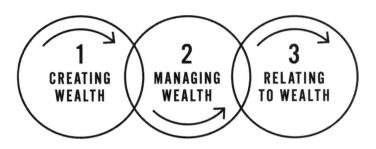

Figure 2.1   Wealth Life Cycle

jealousy if you haven't met your target for building assets on the timeline you expected. You are busy creating wealth and may not have the time, inclination, or knowledge to feel confident managing your assets, while simultaneously feeling insecure about seeking help from outside sources. At this point, you don't know what you don't know.

Phase 1 Example

Steve is a senior engineer at a venture-backed start-up, and his wife, Angie, is a stay-at-home mother. They are in their late twenties, with a growing family, and they are currently focused on building their financial nest egg. Managing their financial life by themselves to this point, they have accumulated bank savings and various retirement accounts of $500,000, and $2 million of vested and unvested stock options. They recently purchased a $600,000 home in a suburb of Boston and enjoy a modest but comfortable lifestyle.

On a typical day, Steve is busy with work demands and Angie is maxed out with two young children underfoot and the house to manage. These obligations leave them with little time to think about their growing cash balance and its impact on their life, other than experiencing less day-to-day stress about having enough money to pay the bills.

Steve and Angie sense that they are on the right trajectory to achieve financial security, but they have a nagging feeling that what they don't know about managing their own money could derail their goals. In fact, they have a real fear of doing something stupid that will create problems. Both attended prestigious universities, and they feel that they should be able to manage their financial life independently given their intellect, education, and the valuable information and services available on the Internet. If they were being honest with themselves and each other, they don't have the time, inclination, or knowledge to think much about finances. Their plate is full right now, with both Steve and Angie working hard and finding time for their family.

As relative newbies to wealth, Steve and Angie have lingering questions that continue to surface in discussions after the kids go to bed, but never seem to get resolved. What's their number for retirement? How much life insurance do they need? Can they afford to purchase that bigger house down the street? When is the best time to start diversifying their options, restricted stock units, or both?

They have considered seeking help from a financial advisor, but there is an inherent fear that they will just be sold products. Even if they wanted to hire an advisor to help, they don't know how to pick one, what to expect, or how much it would cost. It seems that all of their friends who have financial advisors have more money than they do. If only they could find inexpensive help—someone they could trust to educate them on building a financial base.

In Phase 1, your focus should be on educating yourself, becoming aware of common pitfalls and basic financial management needs, and begin the process of vetting a few key advisors you can grow with. Do not overpay or overcommit to advisory services beyond those that will provide more clarity and confidence in your financial life. You are at the stage where your basic financial management needs can be addressed simply and efficiently.

This is the time to find a financial advisor, preferably one with an advanced certification such as Certified Public Accountant (CPA), Certified Financial Planner (CFP), or Chartered Financial Analyst (CFA). These individuals might be working independently or at a wealth management or stock brokerage firm. (For more information about the differences between various advisory roles, see Chapter 3; for links to further information about these designations, see the Appendix.)

Phase 2 of the Wealth Life Cycle involves "Managing Wealth" and all of the decisions, terminology, and strategies that go into overseeing a growing asset base. This can be an overwhelming new task. Wealth creators have plenty of opportunities and choices but often don't have a framework to evaluate the trade-offs, risks, and long-term sustainability of their lifestyle and budget choices. You may wonder:

- Can I afford an advisor, or should I stay on the do-it-yourself (DIY) path?
- How do I find and manage the other professionals I need (attorney, CPA, insurance agent, etc.)?

- How much risk can I afford to take?
- Does the financial equation of my life work in the long term?
- How do I protect my money from loss?
- Do I pay off or pay down debt?
- How does my spending compare to others in my situation? Can we afford a new home or second home?
- What's the best way to pay for my children's education?

Wealth creators in Phase 2 don't want to miss out on an opportunity or make a misstep that will cost them or make them look foolish. They have many people giving them advice, including family and friends, to say nothing of the myriad retail financial services firms seeking their business and offering a bewildering range of products. But they don't know who to trust. And they desperately want and need someone in their life they can trust.

Often, this is a time of great uncertainty, when money starts to have a bigger emotional impact. There is confusion about how to manage the increased complexity of life, and as lifestyle rises to match increased wealth, stress also can increase about whether this is sustainable for the long term. Wealth creators can become hypercontrolling over financial details in this stage because they are fearful of losing the money and sliding backward in terms of lifestyle.

The goal during Phase 2 is to make managing your money as streamlined and seamless as possible, to reduce stress and gain confidence about decision-making, and to start enjoying the benefits of wealth. Engaging help from financial advisors and building a relationship of trust is often a critical step for wealth creators at this stage. During this phase, wealth creators begin pondering the question, "What's the money for?"

Phase 2 Example

Rachael is in her mid-thirties, divorced with two young kids, living in the San Francisco area, and an executive at Apple. She is a high-profile and influential leader managing complex home and work pursuits, with heavy travel, very limited time availability, and a highly scheduled and fast-paced life.

Rachael's net worth, including liquid investments, stock options, and her house, is approximately $10 million, and her annual cash compensation is more than sufficient to cover her lifestyle costs of $300,000 per year, while still materially growing her retirement savings.

Her assets and their associated complexity have grown rapidly over the past several years, and Rachael no longer feels comfortable managing it alone. A broad list of wealth management needs has developed for her, including financial planning, stock option timing and diversification, estate and tax planning, and portfolio management. Rachael recognizes the need to find, manage, and pay for a new team of professional advisors, which she hopes will help her feel more confident and in control of her financial life with limited time, energy, and emotional commitment required from her.

To Rachael, money equals freedom, expanded choices, a mindful focus on interests and passions, and the ability to spend with liberal abandon on experiences and close relationships. However, her lifestyle costs have been creeping higher the past several years, and she doesn't know if her spending is sustainable or how it compares to others in similar circumstances. The volatility of the stock market feels like a rigged game, making her nervous because she doesn't want to go backward and have to earn everything all over again. Does the financial equation of her life work over the long term?

As her affluence has increased, so has Rachael's worry about the entitlement of her kids and the impact that her wealth will have on family and friends. She wants to be viewed by her friends the same way as when she didn't have money. Isolation is building in Rachael's life because there are fewer people in her circle of relationships who can understand the issues and concerns she faces. And, if anything unforeseen happens to her, she doesn't want her kids and family to be burdened or overwhelmed by her money.

This stage of the Wealth Life Cycle is where the management and caretaking of money and the enjoyment of money collide. Just as in business, wealth management can either be done well, creating confidence and clarity toward positive outcomes, or it can be done poorly, creating anxiety, uncertainty, and frustration. The skill and experience of the advisory team you hire will have a huge impact as you navigate through Phase 2, and now is the time to upgrade and expand the advisors you rely on.

Look for a wealth manager to fill the role of "personal chief financial officer" in your life, who understands the scope of your financial picture holistically, assists with communication and coordination of your advisory team, and translates your specific needs into proactive actions that will simplify your life. Typically, you'll find this kind of advisor at a firm that is a Registered Investment Advisor (RIA). (For more information about RIAs, please see Chapter 3.)

Keep in mind that becoming comfortable managing your wealth is a process, so continue to educate yourself and ask questions as you scale this learning curve.

Phase 3 takes the wealth creator on an inner journey of purpose, generosity, and "Relating to Wealth." Truly connecting your values to your wealth is the goal of this phase. When wealth creators feel financially secure and know they can enjoy a certain lifestyle without fear of running out of money, and they have the systems and people in place to manage their money effectively, focus can shift from managing the gift of wealth to maximizing it. Wealth creators want to understand how to have a healthy relationship with their money. They may ask:

Good questions

- What meaning and purpose does my life have (especially if I am no longer working at a high-powered, rewarding career)?
- How do I contribute my time to vocational or avocational work?
- Will money make me happy?
- What place will philanthropy have in my life?
- What does "significance" look like?
- How will wealth affect my marriage or dating life?
- How do I minimize the impacts of affluence on my children?

In Phase 3, wealth creators begin to ask, "What is my life for?" and "How does my money align with and contribute to that outcome?"

How you relate to your money affects all the other relationships in your life. Areas where you and your spouse or partner are not aligned quickly become apparent when addressing the question "What's the money for?" Friendships and family relationships can become strained or uncomfortable when your lifestyle changes and others feel left out, "less than," or jealous.

Some wealth creators feel deeply uncomfortable about their newfound financial freedom because of money lessons ingrained from childhood, and they may even hide their wealth. Your children will feel the effects of your money, and their emotional and developmental well-being is a big concern. We'll examine how the money affects relationships for wealth creators in Chapters 4 and 5.

Many wealth creators want to be proactive in influencing the world around them and the causes they care about through their generosity. They may want to use their money to build a new company or venture that is aligned with something they care deeply about. They also worry about how to leave a legacy, connect their investments to their values, and understand what success looks like—in other words, what is my highest contribution, and why do I exist? We'll examine these questions in depth in Chapters 7, 8, and 9.

When wealth creators can discover the answers to their questions about money and meaning in Phase 3, they are much more likely to avoid the pitfalls of wealth described earlier in this chapter. Their relationships are healthier and they can enjoy the benefits of wealth, while having a higher sense of purpose and connection. In the next chapter, we'll examine the emotional intelligence factors that contribute to or diminish one's ability to be happily wealthy.

Phase 3 Examples

Michael and Amy are a couple in their early forties living in Palo Alto with twin teenage boys. Amy has built a very successful career at Google, and Michael is a partner at a law firm. In addition to having a wide network of friends and family, they are both active in various political and charitable causes.

With a net worth in excess of $20 million, Amy and Michael are confident in the sustainability of their finances and lifestyle. They have become more comfortable anticipating the ebb and flow of rapidly expanding wealth, and they appreciate the opportunities that their wealth presents, both now and in the future. Time freedom is gaining in importance over the pursuit of more money—Michael and Amy want to spend their time exploring their passions and interests more fully, learning how to increase their philanthropic impact, and connecting their investments to social and environment issues they value.

Over the past decade, they've been so busy building and managing their money, as well as the daily details of life, that they haven't made time to think deeply about ideal future outcomes. A few conversations about their long-term goals have surfaced while on vacation, but there hasn't been much incentive to deeply explore and plan for the impact of their wealth.

Michael and Amy have particular concerns about raising their children within the affluence bubble of Silicon Valley, and they worry that their kids will become entitled, or unmotivated to lead a productive life. Tactically, they have thought about setting up trusts and estate plans that limit the flow of assets to their kids, but they are unsure how much of their wealth should go to their sons and when, not to mention other family members.

Amy has toyed with quitting her job and can imagine other careers and adventures that might be invigorating to her life and for her family. She wants to minimize the impact of what she refers to as "the wealth umbilical cord," and instead mindfully design a life oriented toward passions and purpose.

She struggles with making the leap to this passion-driven future because of her own money history: Her father retired early and then floundered, without experiencing much joy. Seeing this negative experience with a close family member has left lingering emotional impacts that Amy must address if she is to find happiness and significance in choosing a different path than the one she is currently on.

Michael really enjoys his work and clients, and the billable hours he generates create a very nice income. However, his financial contribution is dwarfed by the wealth creation from Amy's stock compensation. They have enough money that Michael could easily retire from his law practice, but he has concerns about how this would affect his sons' development. He wants to be a role model for them and help them develop a good work ethic. One the big challenges of Phase 3 for wealth creators is finding meaning and purpose once they've "hit their number" and money is no longer a factor in career decision-making.

Another client experiencing the challenges of Phase 3 of the wealth life cycle is Brady, who sold the profitable entertainment company he was running. He can do anything he wants thanks to this financial windfall, but the money created a scenario where anything was possible and nothing really excited him. Brady has struggled for the past three years with psychological issues around his identity, now that he isn't a well-known producer in Los Angeles anymore.

Pursuing his passion for long-distance running and biking has filled up some of his time, along with short stints mentoring and coaching small business friends, but he still doesn't feel that his life has a real purpose. Brady wants that spark to reignite in his life, but he also doesn't want to go back to the high-pressure and all-consuming time commitment required to build another company. He is still looking for another way to contribute something meaningful.

Megan, the wife of a successful executive, is also struggling to find meaning and purpose in Phase 3 of the Wealth Life Cycle. The size of her and her husband's net worth has mushroomed from single-digit millions to over 20 million in less than five years. Their house and cars are paid for and the kids have gone off to college, with more than ample college savings to go the distance. Vacations are wonderful, dinner out and fun excursions are not a problem, and her husband still works many hours because he loves what he is doing.

Megan, on the other hand, is looking for what to do next, now that the kids have left the nest. She had put her career on hold fifteen years ago to focus entirely on managing the household and raising their children. She now has what she always wanted: time freedom and the health to enjoy it. The question is: Where should she apply her life energy?

Megan tells me that many of her close friends are going through the same life transition, and there is confusion about what to do next, when anything was possible. It is a wake-up call for her to realize that once our wildest financial dreams are met and even surpassed, the need for a new goal emerges. You don't need to focus on building up your savings account because that goal has been checked off, and in many cases, wealth continues to rise materially. What is left are much tougher decisions: Where can I contribute, and how do I find significance?

Wealth creators in Phase 3 of the Wealth Life Cycle often find themselves feeling isolated and unable to confide in others about the complex financial and personal issues they are facing. There are very few people who can really relate to what they are going through. In fact, financial advisors in key positions of trust often don't possess the skill, training, and experience to help them work through these very personal reflections. In Phase 3, there are unexpected blind spots and emotional roadblocks where wealth creators can get stuck.

A wealth coach or other counselor may be needed to help you explore your options and begin to create a life of deeper contribution. Seeking help of this kind isn't a sign of weakness—in fact, many high achievers turn to coaching to give them an edge in various aspects of their lives. The information and assessments in Chapters 7, 8, and 9 of this book will also help you recognize your core values, discover your highest calling, and build the kind of life that many Phase 3 wealth creators are seeking.

What the Wealth Life Cycle Means for You

As we begin our careers, we often have a simplistic view of wealth creation: We will work hard, save and invest wisely, and amass the biggest pile of money we can so we can start enjoying life. The reality is that wealth comes with a great deal of complexity, both practically speaking and in its psychological impacts. Fortunately, the impact and influence that money has on your life evolves in a predictable pattern. Understanding which phase of the Wealth Life Cycle you are in has several benefits:

- It breaks down questions about wealth to a relevant and digestible number.
- It helps you understand the appropriate level of resources and advisory support that you need right where you are.
- It offers insights into both the emotional and practical implications of wealth.
- It provides a road map for what lies ahead as you build wealth, increasing confidence and clarity.

The speed at which you move through the phases of the Wealth Life Cycle is unique to each person and circumstance, and it's not uncommon to have the phases overlap as your knowledge and comfort level with money increases over time. For example, you may be in Phase 1 wealth creation while beginning to grapple with many of the Phase 2 issues of managing your wealth. Likewise, you can become more astute at managing wealth (Phase 2) and simultaneously begin pondering the purposes for your wealth and what kind of legacy impact you want your money to have (Phase 3).

As your wealth grows, understanding and managing its impacts can be overwhelming. The Wealth Life Cycle provides "hand-holds" to move your money and your life forward in a healthy and productive way. In the next chapter, we will review the complications that wealth creates and learn how to traverse this new landscape with confidence.

QUESTIONS TO CONSIDER AS YOU EXPLORE YOUR JOURNEY THROUGH THE WEALTH LIFE CYCLE:

- What do you hope money will allow you to do, experience, contribute?
- Who do you trust and confide in about important financial decisions?
- Where do you need better alignment between your money and your life?

CHAPTER THREE

Navigating Complexity

The starting line for our adult lives is similar for most people—we leave college or graduate school, begin an entry-level job in our chosen profession, and work our way up. When you're a newly minted college grad, life is usually fairly simple: You're dating or perhaps newlywed; you're paying off student debt and saving to buy your first house; you're investing much of your time and energy on building a career, establishing relationships, and enjoying life.

As career success hits and you begin to reap the financial rewards of hard work and a bit of luck, life isn't as straightforward: Job success results in increased responsibilities, longer hours, and more stress; you settle into more committed relationships, including marriage and children, and all the responsibilities that go with those relationships; you begin to acquire big-ticket possessions, such as a home, car, investment property, or "toys" that require time, money, and maintenance. As wealth builds, the stakes grow even higher, and more money equals more opportunities, more choices, and more to worry about. In short: life gets complicated.

Of course, anyone would be grateful to enjoy the security, comforts, and opportunities that accompany financial success; however, as wealth increases, so does complexity. Many wealth creators find themselves confused and overwhelmed as they enter Phase 2 of the Wealth Life Cycle, as discussed in Chapter Two. Complexity is the number one enemy of wealth creators as their assets rise: They are bombarded with decisions they must make and issues they have never faced before.

In this chapter, we'll address many of the practical and emotional implications of increasing wealth. There are unique challenges for wealth creators at this stage, including choosing the right professionals for your team, exploring do-it-yourself (DIY) financial management options versus financial advisors, risk tolerance issues, setting reasonable financial expectations, company stock diversification questions, alternative investments, and socially responsible investing. Before they can make meaning of their money, wealth creators must feel confident in the day-to-day management of their wealth.

I've had literally hundreds of conversations with wealth creators who are navigating a brave new world of complexity. I've listened carefully to their questions and concerns, helping them unpack and understand the new financial management challenges they face, regardless of whether the wealth was created suddenly or over time. Wealth creators need validation that their fears and concerns are normal and solvable: They want to be prepared for what is coming at them, as the game they are playing has just hit highway speeds.

The sections that follow summarize key takeaways from my discussions with wealth creators, providing guideposts for the journey ahead. Depending on where you are in the Wealth Life Cycle, you may find that some topics are vital to your current situation and others are less applicable right now. Wealth creators will face many, if not all, of the challenges addressed in this chapter at some point along their journey through wealth. If certain topics don't seem to apply to you right now, feel free to jump around in this chapter, focusing on the specific issues you are facing as you manage your growing assets.

My Life Just Got More Complicated

Successful wealth creators come to realize the need for a different financial management playbook than when they had $50,000 or $100,000 in a 401k plan, including adding to or upgrading their advisory team. The growing asset base, including various equity and stock option compensation plans, tax issues, and investment and portfolio management decisions, ramps up the level of complexity and time commitment required. What was once something you could look at monthly and make appropriate asset allocation adjustments now needs a higher level of hands-on direction and responsibility. Life and work get busy, and suddenly you find that it's been six months or even longer since you have taken the time to look at your financial reports. As one client said to me, "It's not where I want to spend my time." Another one told me, "I have all the best intentions to review my investment statements when I get home from work, but I just don't get around to it."

You might have been managing your financial life in a DIY approach up to this point, but the growing materiality of your money, as well as the unappealing thought of having to earn it all over again if something went terribly wrong, begin to weigh on your confidence and comfort level. You're at a point where you don't know what you don't know. A founder at a venture-backed start-up told me that he could Google any financial question and look at the top three or four answers, but he could never be sure if the right answer was actually in the fifth or sixth hit—or worse, if he was even asking the right question.

Anxiety around how to best manage your money is understandable because of the vast amount of information regarding financial topics on the Internet and the opaque integration and applicability of that information to your unique circumstances. As one wealth creator stated, "More data and options create uncertainty around what to do and anxiety to make good choices." Another observed that "things are too complex because I can't even do my own taxes anymore."

Specific situations that contribute to that complexity as wealth increases include:

- A broader set of investment products, strategies, pricing and expense structures, and custodial arrangements
- Selecting, coordinating, and communicating with your professional advisors, such as certified public accountants (CPAs), attorneys, insurance agents, and portfolio/wealth managers
- Income tax minimization (e.g., tax loss harvesting, charitable gift planning, stock option exercise timing, retirement planning solutions)
- Risk exposures and coordination (e.g., liability, life and disability, asset protection)
- Illiquid investment alternatives (e.g., private equity, hedge funds, private real estate)
- Wealth transfer strategies, including trusts, family limited liability companies (LLCs), and gifting (note: wealth transfer issues are discussed in detail in Chapter Six)
- Philanthropic strategy and implementation (e.g., foundations, charitable trusts, donor-advised funds)

The scope of these financial management topics can feel overwhelming and dense, yet many wealth creators feel frustrated that they "should" be able to figure it out without help.

They are very smart, have incredible talent, skills, and work experience, and find themselves in the somewhat uncomfortable position of needing guidance and support. I've found that it's a difficult reality for many wealth creators, but most individuals ultimately conclude that professional assistance increases the odds of a better outcome, and they would rather allocate their scarce resources of time and energy to other, higher-value areas of life. The problem isn't brains, but rather having the time, inclination, and knowledge to manage wealth effectively.

Going Solo Isn't an Option

The professionals who support your wealth management needs will directly affect the probability of achieving the best outcomes. A common mistake is to retain the CPA, stockbroker, attorney, and insurance brokerage relationships that you had when you were starting out and had less money. In fact, you may not even have these relationships in place currently, and you will need to fill them from scratch.

As wealth rises, so does the need for a more sophisticated team, and this is not the time to pinch pennies. It's normal to outgrow the capabilities of advisors you had when you were starting out. I often hear things like, "My CPA has been with me since I was in college"; however, that person might be a single practitioner with no expertise in stock option planning, gifting strategies, or other more sophisticated tax and estate matters.

I'm all for giving a chance to your buddy the stockbroker, or the CPA you inherited when your dad retired, but your ability to achieve the best results could be hindered dramatically by advisors who are not experts in managing a larger, more complex pool of assets. If mistakes are made, it can be hard to recover from those losses, and it can set you back years in earning potential. Missing an opportunity because you didn't know about it is just another kind of mistake.

Each member of your professional team (CPA, insurance broker, attorney, wealth advisor, etc.) needs to bring value to you over and above their fee, which includes proactive advice. Too often, I see wealthy individuals settling for an advisory experience that requires them to take the lead in asking the right questions and making suggestions, rather than engaging financial professionals who will proactively lead them to opportunities and advantages. For example, if your CPA completes your tax return in February but hasn't talked to you at all during the tax year she's filing for, you have likely missed out on adjustments and planning opportunities that could have led to a better outcome. You can't afford the cost of a less-than-sophisticated professional advisor on your team.

You might be tempted to take on some of these roles yourself. But just because you are good at creating wealth doesn't mean you have the expertise (not to mention the time) to understand the breadth of issues required to manage it. Often, I see wealth creators clinging to the idea of doing their own taxes, long after they've hired other professionals, perhaps because it's the last bastion of control they think they can have in their financial life. While TurboTax and other accounting software are making it easier to handle simple tax returns, it's really just fool's gold. The reality is that you will miss opportunities to optimize tax savings in a fruitless effort to become a tax expert, and it's just not worth your time. You are a wealth creator—find and hire a qualified professional to help you unless you want your next career to be in accounting.

Make sure that your financial advisors have experience working with clients like you. Ask them about profiles of their typical clients: asset size, complexity, issues faced, specialties of advice. You don't want to be the only large client this person or firm serves, and likewise, you don't want to be a small fish in a very big pond of wealthy clients because you could likely be ignored.

The financial services industry does not precisely define wealth classi-fications, but in practice, you can roughly determine where you stand by calculating your investable liquid assets without factoring in your resi-dence. If that total is below $1–2 million, you would be considered afflu-ent; below $25 million, high net worth; and above that level is the rarified air of ultrahigh net worth. There are firms with asset minimums of $10 million and much, much more. On the lower end, it's common to see a minimum annual fee, or a minimum asset level of $1 million, to even begin working with a wealth manager. These dynamics can make it challenging to understand where you fit in and who might provide the support and experience you need.

Who Can I Trust?

As wealth builds, there is more and more information to process, and the natural reaction is to find and hire a trusted professional to help you with daily money management functions. This process often starts by ask-ing a few close friends in your immediate circle who they work with, and possibly even your CPA or attorney will have recommendations for you to consider. What you will quickly find are many flavors of advice, approaches, philosophies, services, and products. The goal needs to be to find an advi-sor who will sit on your side of the table, putting your interests first. That can become increasingly difficult to discern in the sea of advisory solu-tions you are now swimming in.

It can be difficult to differentiate among all the options because there are many titles used for those who dispense financial advice today: stockbroker, wealth manager, financial consultant, financial planner, and financial advisor, to name a few. At first glance, they all seem to do roughly the same thing and use many of the same words to describe their services.

During the selection and interview process, it will be very important for you to understand where conflicts reside in the potential relationship before moving forward, because there are significant differences between advisory approaches.

In general, conflicts of interest arise when the best interests of the advisor are inherently, or potentially could be, in conflict with your best interests. It's not always immediately obvious where these conflicts lie without flat-out asking potential advisors about them. The most common conflicts of interest arise in how services are priced, including charging commissions for buying investment products like stocks, mutual funds, and annuities, as well as other services like life insurance. They can also be present if the advisor receives incentives from outside vendors for referring and servicing your business. And they may look like additional lines of business, such as tax preparation, banking, and insurance services available to you as a client of the firm. While these bundled solutions can be efficient, you need to be aware of the conflicts created through this type of setup in the name of simplicity and one-stop shopping.

While searching for completely conflict-free advice is an admirable aspiration, it's important to realize that eliminating conflict entirely isn't likely in reality. Forging a trusted relationship is the number one goal. Focus your search on registered investment advisors (RIAs), who are legally bound by a fiduciary mandate (the highest form of professional care), enforced by the Securities and Exchange Commission (SEC), to place client interests ahead of their own. If you find yourself in the brokerage or banking systems looking for financial advice, these tend to be highly sales-oriented platforms that can breed more conflicts because compensation is tied to what is being sold. The professionals within the brokerage and banking systems are only required to maintain a standard of "suitability"—that is, they must make recommendations that are suitable to your personal situation, but their advice does not have to be in your best interest. Suitability standards are only enforced by a self-regulating industry organization.

This is not to say that there aren't many good stockbrokers out there— in fact, I have good friends in the brokerage community, and I would trust them implicitly. But generally, the structure that creates profit for the advisor has an important influence on the relationship. The RIA community isn't perfectly conflict-free, but the structure is a much better framework than usually exists in banking or brokerage houses.

Can't I Just DIY?

Some wealth creators are finding the rise of automated investment platforms to be of great value to them. "Robo-investing" is where a computer

algorithm uses risk tolerance and other factors to determine asset allocation for the portfolio, selects investments, and even rebalances the portfolio periodically to stay in line with specified risk tolerance levels. These
automated platforms typically offer various low-cost investment instruments, such as index funds and exchange-traded funds (ETFs), providing a convenient, minimal-fee option primarily targeted at entry-level
investors.

I'd strongly encourage you not to get sucked into believing that you can
DIY your financial management using these tools beyond an asset base of
a few hundred thousand dollars. Yes, these services are getting more sophisticated all the time, and their value will continue to rise over time. However, as asset levels in your portfolio go up, you hit a point where
computer-driven models no longer suffice. For example, you could have
three or more investment accounts, each needing different investment
strategies, which create conflicting tax outcomes when buying and selling
investments. Customization, coordination, tax implications, and subtleties
surrounding your unique circumstances can only be handled by a trained
human advisor. Calling a 1-800 number will not give you the kind of personalized service you need, and the consequences of making a mistake
with a large sum of money can be devastating.

That said, I am a believer in embracing the best parts of investment auto-
mation, layered with human oversight and wisdom, in what I refer to as a
"bionic solution." Your task will be to look specifically for advisory resources
that take a blended approach, as a way to improve efficiency, cost, and the
investment experience.

It's important to understand that the financial services industry is right
behind the healthcare industry when it comes to how slowly it has embraced
new technologies. Financial services firms often look and feel technologi-
cally outdated and stodgy. It's been an insiders' club and a good ol' boys'
network for a long time, and these old systems are deeply entrenched. However, old systems are being broken down at the fastest pace I've seen in
decades, and that will create wholesale changes in how advisory firms work
with you in the future. Today, you can demand much more from a financial
advisor than your father or grandfather could ask from their advisors, and
the pace of that improvement is increasing every day.

The Need for Sophisticated Advice

The financial services industry has evolved over the course of my career
several times. When I started in the business, its orientation was primarily on money management, and the focus was almost exclusively on picking investments and their performance. Advisory firms then began

including other add-on services like tax and estate planning, insurance reviews, and retirement modeling that generally fit under the financial planning umbrella. These services, combined with money management, have evolved into the wealth management industry we know today, which is holistic in its approach to serving clients' needs beyond just their investments.

Next, the role of a trusted advisor emerged—an experienced guide who fills a quarterback function on your professional advisory team, orchestrating the management of your financial life across various specialists (CPA, attorney, banker, insurance broker, etc.) and disciplines. A trusted advisor is an advocate for the wealth creator, consulting on some of the most important questions of life: Can I safely retire? How much money do I leave my kids? Can we afford a new home? How much can I give away?

The role of a trusted advisor is the antithesis of the algorithms and robo-advisory platforms that can be helpful for those at the DIY stage of investing. Wealth creators in Phases 2 and 3 of the Wealth Life Cycle desperately want and need somebody they can trust, and a wealth advisor fills that personalized role.

As many investment and financial planning services become commoditized through artificial intelligence, the human touch becomes even more valuable. Imagine the emotional impacts of the tidal wave of wealth transfer that is expected to hit the millennial generation over the next 30 years—estimates predict that upward of $50 trillion will change generational hands. Most of these wealth beneficiaries will be unprepared for the impacts on their lives. They will need tactical management of the assets, but more important, they will be seeking advice on the emotional impacts of money.

Wealth creators today want to understand not only how to protect and grow their money, but how the money aligns with their highest contribution and how to have a happy, balanced, and successful life. A coaching or counseling advisory approach offers traditional quantitative wealth management services with an understanding of the life impacts that come with more money and complexity. Wealth creators want to be able to talk to their advisors about topics such as shame and guilt connected with money, identity problems from not finding passion once wealth is achieved, their deep fears of damaging their children due to affluence, and how to find purpose and meaning in wealth.

I recently conducted a wealth counseling session with a financially successful couple from Denver who were dealing with the emotional impacts of their money on their marriage and many other parts of their lives. They had a traditional financial advisor at a well-respected firm who had been managing their assets, but he was ill-equipped to give them the kind of money advice they really needed. We worked together to identify several action steps that would move them forward, negotiating highly sensitive questions around lifestyle comfort levels and clarifying the definitions of several key terms like stewardship. These clients told me, "This is what we cannot get from our wealth manager. This type of help is so much more valuable to us now."

Richard Wagner, the former head of the Financial Planning Association, coined the term "finology," which he defined as the study of the relationship between human beings and money. We are surrounded by this resource in our daily lives, but most of us understand very little about our relationship with money. Marty Kurtz, chief executive officer (CEO) of The Planning Center, says of financial advisors: "We have a higher calling as a profession—being that third party people can discuss money and life with."[24] It's at this precise intersection of money and life that you want to secure competent financial support for the future.

All Fees Aren't Created Equal

You may experience some sticker shock when you decide to engage a wealth manager: it's a wake-up call when you realize that your wealth manager is one of the largest single expense items in your budget. Due to lack of experience, wealth creators often don't know where to turn for help at this transition point from DIY to other alternatives. Understanding what to expect from a financial advisor and how much it will cost can help you move forward with greater confidence.

It seems like a simple question: How much will these services cost me? That depends a great deal on the kind of services and advice you need, which in turn depends on what wealth stratum you're in, making it tough to generalize how much it will cost. Common industry practice is to charge fees as a percentage of assets under management (AUM). This is referred to as "asset-based pricing." Fees are typically charged at 1 percent per year, on the investable assets, and billed quarterly in advance, with the percentage fee declining as asset levels increase. In other words, the more money you have, the lower the percentage charged on the assets you have under management.

The AUM fee structure emerged from the early days of the investment business, where the service provided was exclusively portfolio management—the buying and selling of stocks and bonds. As the financial services industry expanded its scope of services to a more holistic model, the AUM pricing approach was de facto adopted across the board and has seen relatively limited evolution since.

The one-size-fits-all approach of most wealth managers provides a bundle of investment and financial planning services, included in a fee deducted directly from your account each quarter. Giving someone discretionary authority of that nature over your assets can take a bit of getting used to. On the positive side, the advisor has a natural incentive to grow your assets, which then would produce higher and higher quarterly fees as a result. This preliminary sense of alignment is good on one hand because you also want to see your assets rising. It follows that paying more as your money grows feels appropriate. On the other hand, it also incentivizes the wealth manager to advise against withdrawing any assets from your accounts, which in certain circumstances can create a real conflict of interest.

Rory, a software engineer at a start-up in Atlanta, is ready to purchase a new, bigger home for his family and needs to withdraw $250,000 from his investment accounts for the down payment.

Any advice provided by his wealth manager about this financial decision is innately conflicted by the fee arrangement, which means the manager's compensation is reduced if Rory moves forward with the decision. Sadly, I've witnessed many situations where an advisor has strongly discouraged a client from withdrawing money, and the only logical reason for the advice was self-interest.

The other downfall of a strictly AUM pricing approach is that low utilizers of services compensate for high utilizers. Because the fees charged are tied to your assets rather than a specific set of services, two clients that each have $1 million of assets under management will both be charged the same amount of money, regardless of the services provided by the advisor on each account. The client who uses fewer services or makes fewer demands on their advisor's time is offsetting the cost for the client who requires more time and attention.

It's also difficult to measure "success" if all you can look at are numbers on an investment report. When fees are based solely on the investment portfolio, then the attention gets placed there. But that's not the only measure of an advisor relationship. It's almost impossible to unpack how much value you are getting out of other important services like financial planning, or consulting on important financial decisions. In the end, holistically evaluating the merits of an advisory relationship against the fee structure of an AUM approach is very subjective.

Other approaches to pricing such as fixed fees—essentially, an à la carte menu of services with associated cost ranges based on complexity—are becoming more commonplace. The idea behind this approach is that many advisory services require the same amount of time regardless of asset level, or that there is consistency in costs within certain asset-level ranges. For example, the time and cost to complete a college education or retirement planning analysis for clients with anywhere from $500,000 to $2 million in investable assets would be similar. At some firms, this type of approach is being combined with an AUM system for portfolio management, in a hybrid approach to fees.

Wealth creators are increasingly frustrated by fees that are out of touch with their needs and seem excessive when compared to the DIY tools available. They want greater transparency in how fees are calculated and answers to why costs are rising. Both the AUM and fixed-fee approaches are helpful at lower asset levels in keeping the cost conversation relatively simple, but they also are limited in flexibility as wealth increases. With increased assets, there is a demand for a more customized experience and an advisory fee that is based on unique circumstances and needs.

At Highland, we first shifted from charging traditional AUM-based fees to a retainer-oriented structure as a step toward better alignment with client needs and a way to avoid conflicts inherent in the AUM fee system. About three years ago, we went even further and embraced a fully customizable system that begins with understanding client values and needs. We work to craft a set of services that fill those needs, as we define what success looks like for each client. Even clients with similar portfolio asset levels will not have the exact same service offerings and fee structure. Each client has a service offering tailor-made for her or his specific needs, which we review regularly to ensure that we are delivering on the client's expressed values (for example, peace of mind, confidence, or future security for a spouse).

The important outcome from this discussion is to understand the various fee arrangements available today, and then do your homework by comparing and contrasting to find the best alternative for your unique financial situation. While I believe strongly that fees are an area ripe for disruption, there are many advisory firms that are focused on developing new and innovative ways to move toward greater customization when it comes to fees and services.

Once you've assessed your needs, evaluated the various fee structures and breadth of advisory offerings, and assembled a solid financial advisory team, it's time to brush up on some important issues related to investing.

Wealth Creation Versus Money Management

Wealth creation and money management have entirely different objectives, and it's important to understand the difference when setting appropriate expectations around financial results. Investment theory and history tell us that higher risk exposure is correlated with achieving higher returns, and the opposite is also true (lower risk, lower returns). It's common investment knowledge that stock market returns outperform bonds, when viewed over the long term, and that stocks are more volatile in achieving those returns than bonds.

The connection between risk and returns helps us understand the difference between creating wealth and managing it. Tolerance for risk has two components: the emotional tolerance for risk and the practical necessity to accept risk based on the size of your balance sheet.

Wealth creation happens by starting, building, growing, or investing in a business enterprise, whether public or private. Wealth creation activities can also include a concentrated holding or large allocation (relative to the entire portfolio) of a single company's stock, options, or restricted stock units (RSUs), such as Microsoft, Amazon, Apple, Nike, Costco, or others.

When we look at wealth creation from the perspective of risk, there's generally a greater probability of loss associated with the actions involved in creating wealth. This is particularly so if a good chunk of your wealth is tied up in your company's stock, which may be virtually illiquid if you are still working there (more on this later in this chapter). We can look at the tech bubble of 2000 or the 2008 stock market crash for examples of tragic losses for wealth creators, as company stock plummeted from lofty valuations, leaving investors and employees shocked and broke. Wealth creation requires a fairly high tolerance for risk.

Contrast this with the principles of wealth management, which are focused on preservation of capital first and foremost, and then growth of that capital as a secondary objective. To achieve these goals, risk must be lowered, often through diversification and allocation strategies that limit volatility and therefore also lower return expectations.

When wealth creators start to see the results of their efforts, and money starts to accumulate, there is a point where tolerance for risk begins to wane. The "growth-first" mindset shifts to a principal preservation approach. "Just don't lose it" becomes the mantra for advisors to the newly wealthy. It's easy to understand that this anxiety comes from not wanting to slide backward—fear can paralyze your thinking around managing a prudent portfolio. One wealth creator commented to me, "I'm more fearful now because we have further to fall." Another client said, "You know you are set for life, and it's scary to think about that being disrupted."

Jeff, a recent beneficiary of a large stock option grant and exercise, stated that he had "more desire for risk before I reached my number" and feels a clear "shift to being more conservative" now. He adds that if he creates more wealth than he currently has, he could see being more aggressive with some part of it. As wealth increases, there is less and less emotional value assigned to adding more to the money pile, and this is manifested as feeling less tolerant of risk.

In certain situations, maintaining a higher risk portfolio while still working can make sense. Tom took that approach during his early tenure with Amazon. He was comfortable that the stock grants, which were a large part of his compensation, would continue and smooth out any downdrafts in the aggressive liquid investment portfolio he was building. As he has achieved his net worth goals, he is much more interested in throttling back the risk that his portfolio is exposed to. Again, once the target wealth balance is achieved, there is often a bias toward removing risk from the equation.

At other times, it can be hard to rationalize the relatively muted performance from a broadly diversified basket of stocks when compared to a concentrated high-growth stock, rising 15 to 20 percent a year. Sarah, a Microsoft employee with $5 million of stock options and RSUs, was frustrated that her diversified stock portfolio wasn't performing in line with the outsized performance of Microsoft over the past three years.

This is a classic case of confusing a wealth-creating investment in Microsoft with a wealth management goal to lower the probability of loss through diversification. While there hasn't been a real risk of Microsoft stumbling badly or failing in the past few years, there have been long stretches of time where the performance of the stock was well below the market averages, and this is often the case in wealth-creating scenarios.

Clarifying ahead of time whether an opportunity is designed for a wealth creation or wealth management outcome will greatly affect your expectations. It's important to note that funds flow in both directions, from wealth creation to wealth management and vice versa. For example, as a concentrated stock is sold, the resulting portfolio proceeds will typically be managed in a lower-risk money management profile. Most wealth creators see a growing and diversified asset base as an important part of their future financial security.

There are other situations as wealth builds where money is shifted to additional wealth-creating activities, such as exercising and holding company stock and options, buying equity in a business, and purchasing real estate. For example, Steve, a business executive in Austin, Texas, was interested in making a $1 million investment in a commercial real estate opportunity. He should expect excess returns for the concentration and illiquidity risks he is assuming, over other diversified money management alternatives.

There is a clear distinction between emotional tolerance for risk-taking activities and the required level of risk for a particular situation. It's normal to want a safe and sane amount of money that will secure your personal financial needs, but if that becomes an overall-strategy applied to all of your resources, you may artificially restrict your growth potential. Consider setting up separate pools of assets with differing objectives—for example, lifestyle protection assets that are intended to limit volatility and provide security and income, growth assets that will be used for long-term gifting or family objectives, and impact opportunities, where you consciously accept discounted financial returns in lieu of social, environmental, and even spiritual benefits.

Company Stock

As already mentioned, maintaining a concentrated position in your company stock is one of the central ways to create wealth, but it comes with a great deal of risk. It's easy to understand, then, why selling and diversifying your stock, options, and RSUs can be a persistent and compelling thought. You probably have a large portion of your net worth tied up in the company, and your paycheck is also supplied by the same company, amplifying your level of risk.

In my experience, there are three main reasons why wealth creators have problems when it comes to selling company stock:

- **Internal politics and culture.** If you are considered a key executive or employee with "insider status," your stock transactions are public information. Actions you take could have negative impacts on outside investors and employees, and the message being sent by your decision to sell company stock will likely be interpreted negatively unless you communicate the reasons for the transaction appropriately.

    The culture of the company can also materially influence your decision-making around selling company stock. There could be internal pressure to benchmark stock ownership in competition with your colleagues. You could be judged as not being a team player by your boss and others, and as being less fully committed to the mission of the firm than everyone else. What you decide to do with your equity can send unintended messages about your view of the future prospects for the company.

- **Insider trading.** Beyond the internal company politics, you could possess nonpublic information that restricts your practical ability to sell. Insider trading on this type of information is illegal and comes with serious consequences (remember Martha Stewart?), so don't even think about doing it. Corporate counsel and human resource departments for most publicly traded companies will have procedures in place to require authorizations before any stock can be sold if you are considered to be an insider, along with the use of trading windows in which certain transactions can occur safely. These windows typically follow earnings release dates and are not always the best time to sell.

Many sophisticated insiders utilize "trading plans" to navigate these unique challenges effectively. This written plan documents in advance the shares, price, and time targets that will trigger sales. Companies will often disclose these plans to ward off any public relations problems, dampening any unintended external implications.

- **Emotion**. You can get so close to the company's operations and what is going right and wrong that you feel like an expert, and you probably are, to a degree. However, investors don't have your perspective and typically view the company's prospects very differently than the individuals operating it.

  You can also have blind spots that keep you from looking at the company from an unemotional and big-picture standpoint, leading you to justify problems and overinflate future opportunities. Once ego gets involved, it clouds judgment, and this can lead to procrastination or volatile actions. I've seen too many executives bungle their company stock investment by being overconfident or overly negative about their company. Don't let one bad day at the office lead to an irrational stock sale.

  Many years ago, the founder of a newly public company was talking to me about diversifying his stock position. He was resistant to the idea because of the material upside of his large holdings in the company; he expected continuous growth over the coming years. In fact, he told me he would hire a wealth manager once his net worth doubled. On paper, he already had achieved significant financial independence if he took action right then. In that moment, greed took over: The company never hit the targets he was banking on, and the company stock collapsed. This represents a graphic reminder of the importance of harnessing emotions, expectations, and their impact on the ultimate financial result.

Alternative Investments

As your investable assets increase, you may begin to look like a big checkbook for people seeking fresh sources of capital to fund their real estate and private company investments. These early-stage pitches or requests for investors are typically targeted at the friends and family of the founders and will likely increase in frequency over time. For wealth creators, it can be difficult to know if you should get involved, or how much you might invest, and when to say no. The following thoughts are an overview of the practical ramifications and considerations when getting involved in these types of investments, not a critique of the merits of illiquid investments from a portfolio management perspective.

Adding these kinds of investments to your portfolio base is not something you want to dabble in just because you are feeling financially flush. It can be a challenging investment area because it's difficult to gain access to the best opportunities (surprise, surprise—where the best returns live!). It's not easy to evaluate the quality of a deal relative to other options, the minimums required to invest are usually $50,000, $100,000, $250,000 and higher, and there's a time commitment on your part to monitor progress. These factors, along with the added illiquidity, higher fees, increased administrative and tax preparation costs, and the probability of principal loss, make investments of this type more of a gamble.

Where I have seen wealth creators finding success in this space is through their own network of contacts, such as friends from college or previous jobs. Even though these connections are wonderful and possibly can be exploited effectively, tread carefully. It's not that easy to identify the next Howard Schultz knocking on your door, looking for money to fund his small coffee shop. Saying "no" to every opportunity isn't the answer either, because no one wants the dubious distinction of being the guy who turned down an opportunity to invest in a fledgling start-up from the next Jeff Bezos. Truthfully, the landscape of alternative investments is littered with a mind-crushing number of "sure thing" opportunities that flamed out, or at best created uninspiring results for investors. There are exponentially more duds than the handful of success stories everyone fixates on.

Thus, it is critically important to assess the quality of each investment opportunity you are presented with, and that starts with extensive due diligence. In my experience reviewing illiquid investments on behalf of wealth creators for the past twenty-five years, finding a winning formula for a profitable exit is extremely difficult. The wealth creators who have the most success in this area seem to have a nose for people who just flat-out know how to make money. It's not that every investment works out, but their swings at the ball are targeted and meaningful.

Confidence in investing can be gained when you have at least a limited amount of domain expertise in what the company is doing, or your personal relationship with the management team and/or founder convinces you that they have the necessary vision, talent, grit, and track record required to achieve a successful financial exit of some sort. Your relationships are a differentiator that can be mined for value and may prove to be fruitful.

Setting appropriate expectations and not overcommitting financially or emotionally to investment outcomes are crucial to finding success with illiquid assets as well. Pick an amount of money you can afford to lose completely, because the probability of loss points to that as the most likely result. That step can intellectually appear to be easy, but in my experience, when the company goes out of business and your hard-earned money goes "poof," you won't feel so presumptuous about your decision.

Keep in mind that investing at an early stage of a company's lifespan means there will be a need for additional funding if it continues to grow and hit its business targets. Sadly, I've seen people blow their entire wad in a flurry of investment activity, which resulted in poor diversification and the inability to participate in future rounds of financing for the winners. Remember to be judicious in the number of deals you invest in, keeping some dry powder (excess cash) available for the winners you are backing.

One unforeseen consequence of alternative investments can be the time involved in staying connected to a company; reading and assessing updates on its progress; possible advisory board work, including key introductions; and even attending investor status meetings. These investment opportunities can be fun to experience, talk about, and enjoy being a part of something that is creating tremendous energy and hope. It's understandable how a couple of investments can quickly turn into 5–10.

You can start to feel quite brazen in your ability to create wealth in your primary career, which leads to a presumption that you have the ability to do it as an investor, too. I've seen several examples of wealth creators who become heavily invested in start-ups or real estate deals, and then realize how hard it is to make money. Without the skill set needed to thrive in this arena, they end up feeling stuck, overwhelmed with an oppressive time commitment, and with no real way to reverse their decision or extract their investment.

My advice is to keep your commitments to alternative investments very limited relative to your liquid assets until you have the capacity to materially participate (i.e., having a portfolio size north of $10 million and probably closer to $20 million). For a link to an Alternative Investments Primer, please consult the Appendix.

Investing with a Conscience

As your wealth grows, there are increasing opportunities and customization options to connect your money to your values. This area is referred to as "socially responsible investing" (SRI), which is investing with a social conscience. The SRI philosophy looks for opportunities that support a broad array of social concerns, such as reducing negative environmental effects, improving labor relations, and helping underserved communities. At its core, SRI underscores the responsibility of corporations to function as good citizens in the global society.

For many wealth creators, and millennials in particular, investing is not just about making money anymore. Thoughtful consideration of the impact your money can have is included in the equation of wealth building. SRI has been around for several decades, but the trend is gaining momentum. It has grown from being a niche investment idea to attracting enough capital to start having an impact on global challenges at a meaningful scale.

More than $22.8 trillion are invested sustainably, representing more than $1 of every $4 under professional management, according to a 2016 report released by The Forum for Sustainable and Responsible Investment.[25] The intensity of recent growth has been driven by a fundamental shift in how investors and asset owners view environmental, social, and governance (ESG) factors. According to research conducted by the Morgan Stanley Institute for Sustainable Investing, 84 percent of the asset owners surveyed are at least "actively considering" integrating ESG criteria into their investment process, with nearly half already integrating it across all their investment decisions.[26]

Millennials are leading the drive for socially responsible investment opportunities. In a 2017 Factset study, 90 percent of millennials questioned say that they want to direct their allocations toward responsible investments in the next five years. Over 60 percent of millennials expect their wealth management firms to screen investments based on ESG factors. This proportion dips to 53 percent of investors aged 35–54 and only 29 percent of investors age 55 and over.[27]

More important than its potential opportunities and impacts as a trend in the markets, SRI is a way for wealth creators to align their social views and values with their investment assets. In essence, it's an opportunity to reward those companies that contribute to your definition of where society should be headed.

The umbrella of SRI covers many topics and strategies for investing, just as each individual expresses his or her social agenda in a different way. In general, there are three broad strategies for participating in SRI:

- Screening—seeking or excluding companies based on specific social criteria
- Activism—voting proxies and lobbying corporations on specific social issues
- Direct—providing funds to community-level projects and companies, sometimes referred to as "impact investing"

The impact investing strategy of "doing good to do well" is a huge priority for millennial investors and is gaining traction among older investors as well. While it's possible to earn market-rate returns while achieving social impact, investors will likely need to decide what level of concessions on financial results they find acceptable relative to the social value produced by the organization. Even if the odds of healthy returns are slimmer compared to conventional investments, for many wealth creators, value isn't measured only by the bottom line. Depending on an individual's objectives, it can be important to invest not just with your calculator, but also with your conscience.

Managing Philanthropy

There is a saying in giving circles that goes, "You have never met an unhappy generous person." There is plenty of research to confirm that giving has a direct link to happiness and life fulfillment. However, there are practical financial complications associated with charitable giving.

First, you need to understand how much surplus you have available to give. This is one of the benefits of calculating financial "enoughness" for yourself, as discussed in Chapter One. Once you have a handle on your overall spending, saving, and investments, you can better understand your total gifting capacity.

The next questions that arise are whether you intend to give from surplus only, a fixed percentage, or even consider giving away principal over your lifetime or a set number of years. Perhaps you will choose to wait until later in life to dive into serious philanthropy and only focus on building wealth now. "The Giving Pledge," touted by Bill Gates and other billionaires, is a commitment to give a majority of their wealth, except fairly small but meaningful amounts designated for family, to charity. This is an interesting concept to consider for yourself: What impact can my wealth have on the world?

Many people think they will build up a large base of assets and then give it away later in life. This plan results in missing a huge opportunity to feel the joy and satisfaction of giving throughout your lifetime. Research shows we get a little dopamine hit every time we engage in generosity. In general, my experience shows that wealth creators are overly cautious with their resources and miss opportunities to use their wealth for meaningful outcomes earlier in life. If 3 percent is the norm for giving in the U.S. population as a whole,[28] I believe that we have lots of room to push those boundaries of giving much higher without sacrificing our security.

I sat down with a couple recently who had achieved a level of financial success that would cover all of their personal spending needs for their lifetime, with plenty of surplus and contingency. Their assets were around $10 million, and they intended to leave the money to their two children.

However, their stock-based compensation was generating over $1 million per quarter in additional surplus proceeds. They had considered themselves to be very generous in giving to causes up to this point, but they realized that their wealth creation had grown much faster than their giving and spending. They needed a new strategy for giving that included a larger target gift size, to keep pace with their rapidly expanding wealth. They were also struggling with the significant time commitment required to give money away thoughtfully.

If your intention is to give away 3 percent, 10 percent, or more of your income (or assets) each year, and your asset base is relatively modest still, writing checks totaling $5,000 or even $25,000 will not be a significant strain on your time or energy. Heck, you could easily drop $10,000 at a local charity auction on one item, like a fantasy trip to an exotic locale. It requires research and thoughtfulness to give away $500,000, which was the amount we calculated this couple needed to donate to keep their gifting at 5 percent of their assets. How do we even begin to think about giving that kind of money away? To whom? Every year, or every other year?

Even if your giving budget isn't that large, a time investment is still required to properly vet organizations you might wish to donate to. It starts with discussions about specific charities, possibly making site visits to several that interest you, understanding what their needs are and how you might want to fill them. Meeting with donor relations personnel from these organizations can become a full-time job. Determining the most advantageous tax strategy as you make gifts, including appreciated securities, can come with large administrative burdens on you and your professional team in order to complete the gifts.

There are a number of giving vehicles that can assist and add value to the process—everything from the establishment of foundations, donor-advised funds, and charitable trusts of various types. These strategies are extremely valuable tools, but you should take time to evaluate whether they truly meet your needs, because these giving decisions are irrevocable. This is an important decision to discuss with your financial advisor due to the complexity involved. My advice would be not to let the tax tail wag the dog—meaning don't let tactical decisions and tax ramifications overly influence your desire to be generous.

Philanthropic advisors, national and community foundations, groups like Social Venture Partners, and online resources such as Giving Compass.org are available to assist wealth creators in identifying areas of giving that light up your heart while providing due diligence on charitable organizations, information on the latest trends in giving, and much more.

There is also a fairly large administrative component of keeping track of your philanthropy, including monitoring charities' performance, compiling a historical gifts summary for taxes, keeping up with multiyear gift pledges to your alma mater or other organizations, processing stock gifts (which involves paperwork, selecting the security, and deciding on timing), and comparing actual giving to your yearly budget.

Another practical implication of philanthropy is managing the large number of requests you will begin to receive from organizations of all types, from your local firefighters and your kids' school endowment fund to national and international charities. Once you get on a list or attend an auction, you become a candidate for their marketing efforts. It can be overwhelming to sort through the large number of asks, all of them sounding important and worthwhile.

Solving the Complexity Puzzle

You now have insight into many of the practical wealth management issues facing wealth creators. Not every issue will be applicable in your life right now, nor is this intended to be an exhaustive list of the complex issues you might experience as you travel through the Wealth Life Cycle. When wealth creators are overwhelmed with complexity, their experience of wealth can be unhappy, stressful, and even disastrous. On the flip side, learning to navigate the intricacies of wealth confidently and competently will put you light years ahead of most wealth beneficiaries who have to learn the hard way, through painful trial and error.

CONSIDER THE FOLLOWING QUESTIONS AS YOU APPLY WHAT YOU'VE LEARNED ABOUT MANAGING THE COMPLEXITY THAT COMES WITH INCREASED WEALTH:

- What grade would you give your current professional team? What needs do you have that your current team isn't addressing?
- What outcomes would you value most from an advisory relationship? What type of fee structure would align best with your needs?
- What is one thing you could stop doing, or simplify, to enjoy your wealth more fully? (This might include giving up management of your own investments or filing your own taxes, or reducing the number of investments and brokerage accounts you have.)
- Would you like your investments to better reflect your values? If so, how?

CHAPTER FOUR

Money EQ

Those who strive to create wealth through start-ups, real estate, and other successful careers are highly intelligent people, driven to excel in their chosen fields, and often very savvy businesspeople. However, not all wealth creators have a high money EQ—a well-developed emotional intelligence quotient around what money means and how it affects them psychologically.

"Emotional intelligence" (often referred to in shorthand as "EI" or "EQ") is a term created by two researchers—Peter Salovey and John Mayer—and popularized by science journalist Dan Goleman in his 1996 book of the same name. Emotional intelligence involves recognition of one's own emotions, as well as those of other people, and awareness of how emotions can drive one's behavior and affect others. Being emotionally intelligent means being able to manage emotions and their impact, on ourselves and on others. Money tends to elicit strong emotional responses, and appropriately dealing with our emotions around wealth is what I refer to as your "money EQ."

Money History and Relationship

Your relationship with and emotional response to money is strongly connected to your life experiences around it. Understanding and exploring your own emotions about money will help you make healthier decisions around wealth and decrease the potential negative impacts that money can have on you, your relationships, and the world around you.

Money is a huge part of our lives, whether we have a lot or a little, and we are forced to figure out how to deal with money through our experiences. The first place we go when our financial lives get stressful is remembering what we learned growing up. The problem is that most of us don't have a healthy relationship with money, and we weren't taught important lessons about money as kids.

Many of us have never learned basic financial skills, let alone had discussions about an "abundance versus scarcity" mentality, money as a means of achieving important goals rather than money as the goal, the importance of generosity, and the different forms of "currency" that the resources in our life represent. Why would we believe that money can play a positive role in our lives without any training or understanding of what it really means?

Our money history was consciously and unconsciously passed on to us by our parents, regardless of the level of wealth they possessed. Just like passing down family values and holiday traditions, we learn a great deal about our relationship to money from those who raised us, and how they dealt with the opportunities and challenges that money creates. One of the questions I often ask my coaching and wealth management clients is: "What role did money play in your home growing up?" This line of questioning helps reveal the roots of their money EQ.

It nearly always produces a visceral response: A client can almost immediately tell me what was or wasn't discussed about finances; whether mom or dad was frugal, a spender, or didn't ever talk about money; if there was a major financial mistake or investment loss that has haunted the family; or how their parents split up because of money issues and the stress that money represented in their home.

The other interesting outcome of this question is understanding a client's perception of whether she or he was middle class, upper middle class, or even poor. Everyone has clear memories about the quality of the neighborhood they grew up in, whether they had fewer "toys" or possessions than friends, if they had to work for "extras," or if money wasn't an issue and they sensed that, even if it wasn't openly discussed.

A follow-up question I like to ask is: "What lessons about money did you learn that you have taken into your own life?" Again, this question produces immediate and emotional responses such as: Never be in debt, don't trust people with lots of money, never talk about money in public, save everything you can, work hard and be self-sufficient, and "I'll never be poor again." That last statement is the sort of vow that drives career and financial pursuits to obsessive levels because of the fear of not having enough.

The final question in this line of thinking is: "What type of lifestyle do you want for your children?" Again, many people have strong feelings about wanting to provide certain things for their kids, like educational opportunities and sometimes a car, or even a first home. However, it's important to remember that your children may not have sufficient wealth to live the lifestyle you enjoy due to their choices about work and career.

I'll often ask, "Do you want your children to live in your neighborhood?" (By this, I mean, "Do you want your kids to have a lifestyle consistent with what they've grown up with?") What if they can't afford to live in the kind of neighborhood you do? Couples often struggle with the right answers to these questions, and they begin to realize that these are very emotional decisions that they will face sooner than they think.

When we become aware that our emotional responses to wealth are tied to our personal and family history around money, we can see more clearly that our knee-jerk reactions to money matters may not have anything to do with logical decision-making or even our true desires. One wealth creator I worked with named Jane grew up in a household where money was never discussed, but money was always present. She was constantly given more than she needed or even wanted. She recalls her father trying to buy her a new pair of cleats and telling him: "Dad, I don't need another pair of cleats—the ones I have are just fine!"

There was an emotional disconnect between what was being provided— sports lessons, trips, clothes—and what was needed, and the amount being spent. This caused Jane to become extremely frugal and budget conscious as a teenager. Then, when college expenses needed to be paid, her parents took out loans and required Jane to take out loans. The fallout from these money experiences was that as an adult, Jane vowed never to be in debt and to always be in control of her own money.

Another client of mine grew up in a family where money and finances were discussed extensively, including sharing financial difficulties with the children from a very young age. This wasn't a teaching exercise; rather, money was used manipulatively as a method to control behavior, including taking money out of the kids' bank accounts.

The result was a lot of anxiety over money for the members of this family. The message received was that they should try to accumulate as much money as possible, as quickly as possible, so they could be in control of their own lives and no one would have the power to manipulate them. This resulted in an extreme drive to build and create wealth so no one would ever be able to hurt them financially again.

My wife, Kelle, and I have also witnessed how our individual family money histories have played out in our adult lives. I came from a home where my parents were very frugal about money, while Kelle had parents who bought her a cool car in high school and went on lots of family trips, even though this free-wheeling spending created stress in their home. Kelle was in debt when I met her and didn't have a healthy relationship with money. Meanwhile, I was hyperfocused on making money so I could buy the things that eluded me as a younger person, and I knew that if I wanted something, I had to earn it.

The incongruence of our different upbringings and comfort level with money came into play as we raised our family. We purchased homes beyond our financial means, and our desire to give our kids every opportunity meant prioritizing private school education and private lessons in everything from baseball to piano, even though it stretched our financial capacity, and money worries added greatly to our marital stress.

Examining your own money history can help you increase your money EQ. As you become aware of the experiences and history behind your relationship with money, you become empowered to change unhealthy behavior. Having a high money EQ includes becoming self-aware and making financial decisions about wealth based on a solid understanding of how you feel about money and why you feel that way.

Shame and Guilt around Money

Underneath the excitement and privilege that new wealth brings are dark and sinister feelings that can creep into our psyche and negatively influence our thinking about money, and ultimately our happiness. Shame and guilt are fear-based critics that bombard our minds with messages like: "You're not good enough," "You don't deserve it," "You're a rich snob," or "They don't really like you for you, just your money." The natural response to pain of this sort is to cover it up with busyness, hiding, control, and many other coping behaviors.

Some wealth creators narrow their circle of relationships to include only those who have achieved a similar level of wealth, so they won't have to experience any worry about being judged or shamed for their financial status. Shame and guilt about having "too much" or more than those around you is a real challenge faced by many wealth creators. It's important to find an outlet to share these feelings, but that can prove challenging when relatively few people really understand what you are going through and might judge you for even having these feelings.

A very wealthy woman I worked with several years ago was living in luxury and was anxious about her grand lifestyle relative to her lower-income colleagues and the customers she served. What if they found out how she really lived when she wasn't at work? The paradox of her pampered life made her feel uncomfortable about her wealth at times, and she was having a hard time enjoying her affluence.

Should she deny herself things that she could easily afford in favor of a more spartan lifestyle in order to fit in better at work? Could she do more to help the less fortunate, in the hope that charitable giving might curb the nagging feelings of inequity she experienced daily? As we sat in the living room of her mansion, I could sense the tension she was experiencing and her embarrassment in sharing these very personal feelings, and yet she needed to be validated and understood.

In another case, a single woman didn't want anyone to know she was wealthy because it affected her ability to build meaningful relationships with men. Once her romantic partners found out about the money, it changed how they acted toward her, and she was frustrated and ashamed about that fact. She just wanted to be loved for who she was, not because she was rich. For that reason, she began keeping her wealth a secret and went to great lengths to ensure that only a very short list of people knew the truth about her financial status.

Regret and jealousy are cousins of money shame and guilt. Regret can be caused by the new challenges and changes to your life caused by wealth: You find yourself wishing at times that you could roll the clock back to a simpler time, before the money made everything more complicated. The other form of regret is caused by poor or suboptimal financial choices and decisions when viewed in hindsight. You find yourself saying, "If only. . . . ." Many times, these perceived failures can drive unhealthy future behaviors around money accumulation.

Jealousy creeps in when you start comparing what other people have accumulated or the success they've achieved to your financial position in life. No matter how financially successful you are, there will always be someone with a bigger house, a fancier car, and a larger bank account than you. Have you ever found yourself in a situation where everyone wants to talk to the successful entrepreneur or wealth creator at the party and looks past you during conversations? It's easy to understand how the definition of success has been built using the scale of money and possessions.

Part of increasing your money EQ is acknowledging and understanding these darker feelings about money and wealth, including guilt, shame, regret, and jealousy. Having someone with whom to explore these feelings and uncertainties, whether an advisor, a therapist, a friend or family member, is important.

I call this role the "Wealth Confidant"—part financial guru, part coach, this person ideally should be able to consult with you about money matters and the life circumstances that money influences and impacts. This relationship represents the highest form of trust because you'll share the intimate details of both your financial life and your emotional life with him or her. It's the reason I call my podcast *The Wealth Confidant,* and it's the role I play for my clients.

Scarcity Versus Abundance

I wanted a way to understand and assess the various emotional responses to money that I was hearing and experiencing from my clients. In compiling the data I had gathered from these conversations, I found that wealth creators tend to be located somewhere along two different continuums when it comes to their money EQ: their level of abundance versus scarcity thinking and their spectrum of ownership versus stewardship thinking.

Scarcity thinking can make one feel like there is never enough money (or time) available and the only solution is to get more. Both of these commodities (money and time) are valuable to wealth creators, and more money begets more time and choices, so the focus tends to stay on amassing more money. Scarcity thinking forces a type of win/lose scenario: There are limited resources with only so much available—if someone else gets it first, there won't be any left for me.

Just reading that statement, you can probably sense the fear and anxiety created by this mentality. This mindset creates a lot of negative energy around capturing more and more financial resources. It's almost like playing the children's game of musical chairs: Scarcity thinkers are constantly going around a circle of chairs where there isn't a spot for everyone, and they definitely don't want to be the person left without a seat. Scarcity thinking leads to a myopic form of money attention-deficit disorder: When there is never enough, you never get to relax and enjoy what you already have.

Abundance thinking is the opposite of scarcity—it's a mindset that believes there is more than enough available for everyone, and I will get my share. This mindset does away with the fear and worry around not having enough chairs for everyone to have a seat at the table. It doesn't mean that you don't believe in working hard to earn your share and being very intentional about that, but the underlying feeling is that there is plenty available. There is enough for my current circumstances, and additional financial resources will be available to me in the future as I need them. Having an abundance mentality moves the needle on our money fuel tank to "Full," where we can experience feelings of contentment, satisfaction, and calm.

Albert Einstein proved that everything is energy (literally). Bruce Schneider, founder of the Institute for Professional Excellence in Coaching (iPEC), teaches that people produce two types of energy: catabolic and anabolic. Catabolic is draining, contracting, and resisting energy. In the simplest form, it represents stress, and when we are exposed to stress long enough, it causes of all kinds of health and emotional problems. Catabolic processes drain the body's store of energy. Anabolic energy is constructive, expanding, and rejuvenating energy, and it is the process by which the body builds itself up and grows.[29]

These concepts are a useful way of understanding abundance and scarcity mentalities. Similar to the way catabolic energy use drains us, scarcity thinkers believe they can only gain something at your expense. Abundance thinking is like anabolic energy, centered on creation and focused on expansiveness. Wealth creators who want to increase their money EQ can learn to shift their focus toward abundance rather than scarcity thinking.

Ownership Versus Stewardship

The other scale I like to measure with wealth creators is their level of ownership versus stewardship thinking. This way of thinking relates to how you hold the money: open-handed or closed-fisted. If, metaphorically, your hands are closed tight around money (and many times, they seem to be holding on to it for dear life), this is an ownership response. The money is mine; I earned it; it's for my benefit and my benefit only. When we ask "What's the money for?" the answer for those with an ownership mentality is there isn't any purpose for wealth beyond myself and my own needs.

Several years ago, I worked with a highly compensated executive in an international professional services firm. Scott was singularly focused on the size and growth rate of his net worth and the lifestyle benefits that then would accrue to him. Periodically, I would invite him into a conversation to explore a larger definition regarding the money's purpose, but he wanted no part of it. He told me in no uncertain terms, "Look, this is really simple: I view the money exclusively for my benefit, and to share some with my kids and a few close friends, period."

He was very pragmatic about his daily grind to create and compound his wealth, anticipating reaching higher and higher levels of assets that would then expanded his lifestyle options. Developing a sustainable retirement cash flow from what he "owned" is what brought him energy and comfort. In a nutshell, his life formula was: Work hard and enjoy the money to the fullest. For Scott, the purpose of wealth was solely to benefit himself, and perhaps his closest family members.

At the extreme, an ownership mindset hijacks our emotional response to money and taps into a Gordon Gekko (from the movie *Wall Street*) "greed is good" mentality, where our focus is primarily on selfish outcomes. Just like a kid at Halloween going door to door collecting candy in a pillow-case, the game is getting as much as you can, with no intention to share it with anyone. Many of the pitfalls of wealth discussed in Chapter Two—increased isolation, depression, self-centeredness, anxiety—spring from an ownership response to money.

On the other hand, a stewardship mindset believes that money flows through one's life like water, as Lynne Twist describes in her book *The Soul of Money*. She writes, "Money flows through all our lives, sometimes like a rushing river, and sometimes like a trickle. . . . it can purify, cleanse, create growth, and nourish. But when it is blocked or held too long, it can grow stagnant and toxic to those withholding or hoarding it."[30]

The role of a steward is to manage or care for resources entrusted to him. A steward is a fiduciary, which is the role I play as a wealth advisor. The money isn't mine, but I am required by law to treat the money with the same care as if it were, and push my own self-interest to the background. In a stewardship mentality, we think of "my" money more like "ours"—owned by someone else, and we are just watching over it and using it for a time. We all realize that "you can't take it with you," which means that we have an opportunity to reframe money as something different: a resource that we borrow and enjoy for a time rather than something we hoard and hide. Think of wealth as energy—a resource that we don't own, but that can be put to use for the greatest good in our own lives and those of others.

Kevin and Carole, a couple who experienced significant windfalls from Carole's executive roles at two high-growth companies, engaged me to help them balance the need to tap assets for retirement spending while living out their faith-based commitment to steward what they saw as God-given resources. Their perspective was that they were entrusted to enjoy, protect, and grow these assets, but the money was not exclusively for their benefit. Kevin and Carole's top priority was generosity: After giving modest gifts to their children, they wanted to contribute all of the remainder of their assets to philanthropic causes and their church.

This couple embodied a stewardship versus an ownership mindset. In my role as a financial advisor, it's typical to exclude homes, boats, and personal property from calculations regarding financial independence as a qualifying simplification. With Kevin and Carole, they made it clear that they wanted to put all of their assets into the pot for calculation purposes, honoring their belief that they were simply stewards of these resources. Each year, we would rerun our financial independence calculations—not to determine how much of their wealth they needed to keep, but how much they could give away!

Stewardship thinking leads to the emotional response of generosity and sharing for the good of the whole, not just myself. Giving is money dopamine, and it can produce an emotional high and feelings of joy. The old saying, "You have never met an unhappy generous person" is a truism. Developing a stewardship relationship with your money is key to increasing your money EQ and protecting yourself and your family from the pitfalls and risk factors associated with wealth.

Conscious Versus Unconscious Money

In a stewardship mindset, we are conscious of the choices we make about the resources put in our care, whether those resources are our time and talents, environmental or natural resources, or the dollars we have in our bank accounts. I have realized how unconscious I am in many areas of my life (for example, not being educated about the harmful effects that my consumption has on the planet, from the waste I produce to the chemicals in my food). As I become more aware of these issues, it is harder and harder for me to go back to a place of relative ignorance.

The same concept applies to our money itself: We can be aware of where it is, what it is invested in, and how we are using it to support and contribute to both solutions and problems in the world. Alternatively, it can be easy to take the unconscious route: We invest on autopilot, without considering the downstream effects our money can have when we support companies and products that cause harm or those that do good. Not allowing money to flow where it needs to go can be another form of unconsciousness. For example, if I hoard monetary resources because I don't want to put in the time or energy toward understanding where they could do the most good, I can avoid my responsibility as a steward of those resources.

Our level of money consciousness versus unconsciousness can also apply to our money EQ. By examining our family's financial history, our beliefs, our training, and our deepest fears related to money, we suddenly gain consciousness of our money motivations and impulses. Instead of unconsciously blundering through the experience of wealth, we can increase our money EQ, which leads to wiser decisions and greater happiness in our financial lives.

Joel Solomon, cofounder of Canada's largest mission venture capital firm, Renewal Funds, offers this advice on becoming conscious in his book

The Clean Money Revolution: "Do business and investments the same way you do food and personal health. You are what you eat, and you are what you invest in. The side effects of how we make money live in us."

Joel adds: "We are our money. It has our name on it. . . . How we use money is an expression of who we are and all that we believe."[31]

Money represents the calling card of our priorities, our values, and our choices. Think about your money as if each dollar bill has your name written on it: How does that accountability change your decisions around money? Raising our consciousness level about the financial choices we make is an important step in healing our relationship with money and increasing our money EQ.

Money EQ Assessment

My goal is to help wealth creators become more conscious of their emotional responses to money, especially given their particular money history and how it plays out in their current relationship to money and wealth. The Money EQ Assessment provides a framework for understanding how and why you are feeling the way you do, as well as an assurance that your feelings about wealth are normal. Examining where you fit within the four areas of money EQ can open pathways to understanding and begin a healthier emotional relationship with money. I believe that shifting toward an abundance/stewardship mindset starts by changing our thinking about money, which leads to changes in our emotions and feelings about money, and ultimately, this will change our actions around money.

There are four Cs that represent four areas of thinking and feeling in the Money EQ Assessment: Concern, Caution, Control, and Content.

The first quadrant, **Concern,** is grounded in a scarcity and ownership mindset. Those experiencing "Concern" as their emotional reaction to money have a tight-fisted response, coupled with a scarcity mindset of always needing more money. The range of emotions in this quadrant includes worry, anxiety, anger, and even obsessing over money, including overfocusing on accumulation. There is a feeling of jealousy about what others have and the belief that what I have is not enough.

"Concerned" wealth creators need more money to feel safe and independent and to enjoy the life they've envisioned. Their focus is constantly on building and preserving lifestyle resources, with the hope of pushing back the ever-present fear and stress that something could go wrong, forcing retreat or downsizing. Catabolic and draining energy is at its highest level here.

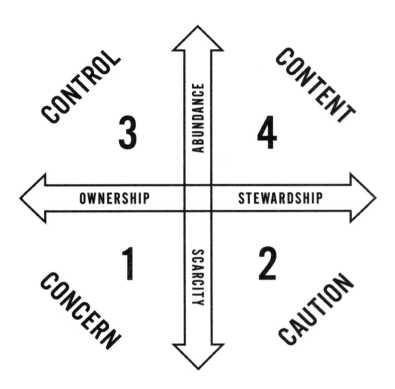

Figure 4.1   Money EQ

Kate, an early employee of a very successful technology company, was comfortably retired with a beautiful home, vacation property, and elegant lifestyle, all built on the strength of company stock, which had grown materially over the years and represented security and safety. The amount of stock far exceeded her personal spending needs, even when projected into the future. However, Kate was emotionally hamstrung by her ownership of this stock—even the thought of selling off some of it to diversify her portfolio created significant stress.

While she knew intellectually that her assets were more than enough to cover her needs, Kate was petrified of any real or potential disruption of her lifestyle and comfort. Anything that looked remotely like risk was avoided. She needed constant reassurance that the excess margin was continually growing and providing a sufficient buffer to withstand any seen or unfore-seen shocks. It seemed like there was no amount of money that could take away her fear. Kate exemplifies the "Concern" response to money.

Looking at the second quadrant in the Money EQ Assessment, **Caution,** we shift to a stewardship mindset of "ours" and an open-handed approach to money, while continuing to experience the stress associated with scar-city and feeling that you still don't have enough. Cautious behavior reigns because of the conflict that develops between the impulse to conserve and protect what you have and still attempt to appreciate the gift that money represents.

This friction may cause you to justify selfish behaviors that lead to feel-ings of regret and disappointment, resulting in a desire to be more priority-based and trusting. Shame associated with a poor history of financial decisions, or jealousy from watching the success of others, can also land you in this zone, where you feel that you deserve a different outcome than what is present in your circumstances and don't understand why you have not achieved it.

Lance has a sincere desire to be a good steward of the blessings in his life, and he has a lot to be thankful for. He believes strongly that life is a gift, and so are his financial resources. Living in an expensive suburb of Denver, he is diligent about making responsible spending decisions, while splurging every so often to enjoy the fruits of his earnings. In reflective moments, Lance has shared with me that he is more than a little bit anx-ious about the future and whether he has enough money saved from his high-paying job.

He wants to let go of fear and be open-handed with his money when presented with opportunities to apply it for a higher purpose, but that can conflict with his need to feel financially safe. Specifically, he wants to increase his level of giving to church and charity, but he often finds those desires overruled by fear and worry about future security, which lead him to take the safe route of doing nothing or doing much less that he would like. Lance is in the emotional space of "Caution" when it comes to money.

The third quadrant is **Control,** where the ownership and abundance mindsets meet. You have a clear sense that you have enough, and maybe even more than enough, but your purpose for money is focused almost exclusively on your own security and self-sufficiency. Whatever you have is yours—you worked hard for it, and you plan to enjoy it. This intersec-tion of attitudes can lead to overconsumption, hoarding, and arrogance in the belief that you deserve a certain lifestyle.

Those experiencing a "Control" response can get stuck thinking obsessively about money, experiencing feelings of guilt, or trying to avoid introspection about their attitudes and actions. In relationships, those in the "Control" quadrant may find themselves unable to address emotional and communication issues with a spouse or partner around alignment of priorities. Avoidance and an attitude of "I don't want to deal with it" or "I don't know how to deal with it" obstruct the flow of money and can create a state of emotional constipation.

Bryan has both a mindset and financial statement that displays "plenty." He lives a very comfortable life, with all the accoutrements of monetary success: a house in the right ZIP code, a luxury car, and an unlimited food, wine, and travel budget. He wants for nothing materially, and in terms of financial stability, his life is essentially on cruise control.

Even though Bryan doesn't spend a lot of time worrying, he is primarily concerned with avoiding any risks that would affect his quality of life. There is a nagging sense that he would like to be more generous with and focused on others sometime in the future, but for now, he enjoys splurging on himself. He believes there will be a time for more intentional purposes later. Bryan displays the strong ownership mindset associated with "Control," and he may someday move toward abundance.

The final quadrant, **Content,** is the marriage of abundance and stewardship, which creates connection and alignment with your money. The open hand of stewardship and understanding a higher purpose for the money is coupled with a mindset of abundance and sufficiency that allows money to flow freely and confidently throughout your life. Those who are "Content" emotionally understand the connection between purpose and money. Their sense of a higher calling generates a freedom from fear that spawns contribution and generosity in meaningful ways.

An example in the area of "Content" is difficult to produce because no one is a saint when it comes to money. In thinking about someone to write about who embodies the qualities of contentment, I decided to describe one of the most generous people I know. Becca never worked toward the goal of being rich, and she exudes a gentle sense of confidence that she will have sufficient financial resources to meet her needs, regardless of the circumstances. She already feels excessively blessed, and that feeling is not based on her investment statement balances. She has pursued career objectives from a place of purpose and calling, believing that she has a responsibility to use her gifts and financial resources as a steward would, both to enjoy life and to support the issues in the world she cares most about. She is proactive in seeking opportunities to be generous, giving large, sustaining amounts to organizations or as little as a $20 gift to a stranger in need. She doesn't just give money—she also wants to be generous with her labor, influence, and expertise. Becca feels "Content" and free in her relationship with the money because of her open-handed attitude to those less fortunate, as well as a focus on meaning and abundance rather than consumption.

Because money and life are challenging and always changing, you may experience shifts from one quadrant to another as life circumstances affect your emotional development. I believe that your money EQ can evolve and mature through self-awareness; however, you may experience triggering events that cause you to revert to old ways of thinking and behaving. For example, when the market drops and financial projections look less rosy, it can be easy to feel less confident and generous. It's helpful to take an emotional inventory, to evaluate your sense of abundance and stewardship and orient your thinking toward a more confident, connected financial future.

In my own life, I want to experience more contentment in my money EQ, but I am often distracted by my own fear-based self-focus and feelings of scarcity. Sometimes the emotional need for "more" comes from within, and sometimes our consumption culture looks awfully appealing. I've become much more aware that I am truly in control of my thoughts relating to money. The more I consciously orient my thoughts toward anabolic and life-giving ideas, the less control, concern, and cautionary emotions and behaviors surface, and the more joy and contentment I experience.

For me, this means trusting in God that sufficient resources will be supplied to meet my needs, recognizing that I have incredible abundance when compared to most people in the world, and accepting that I must act as a steward of these resources and gifts in my life. In my case, I believe that God has a purpose for these resources that goes beyond my exclusive personal consumption, and I experience great joy when they are put into motion and aligned with my unique contributions and calling, subjects that we will explore in later chapters.

To help you understand your own ownership/stewardship and scarcity/abundance responses to wealth, I've created an online interactive tool for wealth creators, called the Money EQ Assessment. When you visit the link, you will be asked questions intended to uncover your emotional responses to the concepts of stewardship and abundance.

Your money EQ isn't a number. It is a set of emotions related to money that drive your behaviors concerning money. Some of us sail through decisions concerning money with confidence, while others struggle. Each of us has a unique emotional relationship with money—one that is influenced by a host of attitudes, opinions, and past experiences. These combined elements predispose us to living a life where money works in a positive way to achieve our goals, or money works against us, leaving us feeling uncomfortable or unfulfilled.

I invite you to take the Money EQ Assessment online (http://www .jcchristianson.com/assessment) and gain a better understanding of your own emotional intelligence when it comes to money.

QUESTIONS TO CONSIDER AS YOU EXPLORE YOUR MONEY EQ:

- What lessons about money did you learn as a child that you have brought into your adult life?
- Are you conscious about your money, or do you choose to ignore it? Why?
- What's one thing you would like to change about how your money makes you feel or act?

CHAPTER FIVE

Navigating Relationship Roadblocks

It's a fact: Our lives work better when our most treasured family and friend relationships are healthy and positive. Likewise, the relationship you have with money, while not a person, greatly influences these relationships, and ultimately your life satisfaction. At the intersection of money and relationships are emotional pressure points that can be sources of fear, worry, and anxiety. These can become roadblocks and "stuck" areas for wealth creators. If left unattended or ignored, these challenges often become acute problems that linger and create great unhappiness for the long haul.

My work with first-generation wealth creators shows that it is difficult to anticipate these potential stressors when you have limited money knowledge and experience. Your money EQ is intimately tied to your personal money history, and if the experience of wealth is new to you, there is a lot to learn. In this chapter, we'll examine some common money roadblocks where people get stuck, influencing and altering their relationships. It could be that your relationship to the money that is keeping you stuck. It could be that your definition of success needs to change.

We will explore particular issues related to marriage and money, such as financial roles, spending and saving decisions, determining priorities, values alignment, and "my money" versus "our money." By understanding the areas that are the main culprits of financial stress for wealth-creator couples and learning how others have navigated them successfully, you can improve your overall financial and relational well-being.

New wealth also can change and challenge relationships with family members and friends. Some of the issues that arise include jealousy, intimidation, expectations around paying for things or offering financial support, and simply growing apart because of the financial divide. Many wealth creators try to protect their relationships by hiding their financial status, which can also cause emotional roadblocks.

Marriage, Relationships, and Money

Those closest to us—our spouses or partners, the ones we love most—are heavily affected by our money and how we communicate about it, or don't. "Money issues are often denied, overlooked, or ignored in courtship, argued about constantly in marriage, and the focus of many divorce proceedings,"[32] writes professor Adrian Furnham. Money is one of the most challenging subjects for marriages and relationships in general, and the main culprit for divorce and marital stress.

In a study conducted in 2013 using data from over 4,500 couples, researchers found that arguing about money was the top predictor of divorce. "It's not children, sex, in-laws, or anything else," says Sonya Britt, assistant professor of family studies at Kansas State University. "It's money—for both men and women. Results revealed it didn't matter how much you made or how much you were worth. Arguments about money are the top predictor for divorce because it happens at all levels."[33]

Writing in the *American Journal of Family Therapy,* Joan Atwood notes, "Speaking about money in marriage is the last taboo. Couples would prefer to talk about sex or infidelities rather than how they handle family finances or how much money they earn."[34] And a 2014 poll conducted by *Money* magazine found that 70 percent of married couples argue about money—more than any other topic.[35]

In my experience, there is no more volatile and divisive subject than money in a relationship. We all have a unique relationship with money that we bring into marriage, friendships, and family situations. I'm not immune myself: My wife, Kelle, and I can get into tense discussions about differences in spending decisions, how much and when to provide support to our kids, and how much we should be saving for retirement.

What I've learned over many years of counseling with couples about money is that open, nonjudgmental communication is the key to resolving most issues, including those around financial roles, saving versus spending, financial priorities, values and money "ownership."

Role Decisions

Who is going to manage the family finances is an important decision for couples. In my experience, one partner is usually delegated this responsibility because of prior experience or general interest. However, while the other partner can feel relieved not to have the day-to-day burden of keeping track of the finances, this can be a scary and vulnerable spot to be in when disagreements over money crop up.

Jake and Amanda faced the roadblock of financial roles in their marriage as their wealth increased. Jake was a successful executive and rose up the corporate ladder quickly to a position of significant authority. He worked all the time and was free with his spending on homes, travel, and lifestyle. Jake didn't give much thought to saving or controlling their spending because the money was flowing in, and he really didn't have time to think much about it. He came from a background with very little money, and he didn't really understand money or how to manage it. His wife was busy raising their young family, and Jake had loosely taken over the responsibility of paying bills and dealing with their financial life.

Amanda had become accustomed to the luxurious lifestyle afforded by their income, but realized that if anything ever happened to Jake, she would be in a frighteningly vulnerable position, completely ignorant about their finances. This created a great deal of stress for her. She was panicked that she would be left alone with small children and the obligations of an expensive lifestyle, with no real understanding of how the financial parts fit together. My suggestion to help Amanda feel more comfortable was for this couple to switch roles and have her take over paying the family bills. In this way, Amanda could become familiar with the various day-to-day financial needs of their family.

For many new wealth beneficiaries, the extensive array of employee benefits (insurance, stock options, etc.) they receive, along with debt arrangements and normal household bills, can be overwhelming as the financial complexity of their lives increases. I've found that it can be helpful to rotate the responsibility of "chief financial officer" in the family to each partner periodically, for three reasons:

- It's easy to lose sight of the details of your financial life. There's nothing like becoming immersed in the actual bills and accounts, and getting to know the professionals who service those accounts, to feel more empowered.
- You might have a different perspective on financial commitments and strategies than your partner does, and your fresh ideas could inspire a new approach.
- It gives each partner in the relationship an opportunity to appreciate the time, energy, and responsibility that this role requires.

For Jake and Amanda, changing roles had a great impact. Amanda felt empowered by her new understanding of their financial picture, and her stress around the future was relieved.

Spending and Saving

Determining the level of spending and saving for the family, which determines the lifestyle you want to have, can be fraught with tension. The family budget has a tendency to move up in tandem as the asset level rises, and the questions become "Where does that stop?" and "What can we afford?" I see differing views on these questions frequently, as one partner pushes for more luxury and the other partner is more conservative and frugal. It's rare that both partners in a relationship have similar positions on determining spending.

Each partner or spouse has their own money history they bring to the relationship. Spending comes with triggering messages from parents and other caregivers that can greatly influence our decisions. For example, if you grew up in a household where finances were tight and your parents only bought items on sale or with coupons, you learned that spending must be tightly controlled and you should always try to get the best deal on a purchase. Or you may have been raised in a household where the message was "Don't show that you have money," which meant keeping your lifestyle understated and making spending decisions to ensure that you will blend in with the crowd.

For wealth creators, there often isn't a clear benchmark for what level of lifestyle is desirable or appropriate. A common question I hear is, "How does our spending compare with other people in our situation?" Basically, couples want to know, "Are we OK? Are we normal?" Because the total amount of their spending is a lot more than they've ever spent before.

This can be a particular issue in wealth bubbles, such as Silicon Valley or Seattle, where everyone is a "millionaire" and the basic cost of living is very high. "People around here, if they have $2 or $3 million, they don't feel secure," says David W. Hettig, an estate planner based in Menlo Park, California. "We're in such a rarefied environment, people here lose perspective on what the rest of the world looks like." David Koblas, a Silicon Valley computer programmer, describes this as "upsizing your life to your cash flow."[36] When everyone around you owns a car worth six figures and sends their kids to private schools, and the average house costs over a million dollars, it can become difficult to set an appropriate benchmark for spending.

In general, I've found that a lot of pressure can be relieved when there is quantitative clarity about whether the lifestyle chosen is sustainable over the long term. Constantly questioning whether the money will be sufficient for your future is very unsettling, and it causes a lot of stress within relationships.

For Steve and Sally, recent beneficiaries of a very lucrative family business sale, there was a significant increase in lifestyle spending that occurred over several years. Sally had grown increasingly uncomfortable with their spending levels. She was raised with a financial message that said to keep quiet about money and keep your lifestyle understated. She became visibly stressed when she spoke about their expensive home, fancy cars, and the opulent travel they were experiencing. It wasn't that she didn't enjoy all those things, but it made her very uncomfortable that others might think of her as rich. She longed to live in the simpler version of their life, pre-business sale.

Steve also had the feeling that their spending was excessive at times, but he didn't want to give up the power to splurge on cars, clothes, and other luxuries when he desired. He realized that there was significant friction with his wife about reducing expenses. Sally just wanted to know there was a budget they agreed upon, and that there would be accountability to stay within it and not deviate. She had lost confidence in their ability to determine an appropriate level of lifestyle spending and then live within that amount.

It's a statement I hear often when people are faced with the reality that they are spending $250,000 annually, and sometimes much more. "Where does all that money go, because it doesn't feel like we are doing that much?" This statement is partly true because it does cost a lot to maintain the homes, cars, and experiences of a higher lifestyle, and it can sometimes feel like couples are just paying for the choices they have already made and not doing anything extra.

To help this couple reconcile their differences when it came to spending and saving, I began by asking Sally to describe the lifestyle that would make her comfortable. It included a smaller home (but still in a nice neighborhood) and getting a clear picture of what their needs were versus wants on the expense side. Sally needed to know that they would stay accountable to that number by talking about it regularly, and thus confidence in each other's financial decisions could be built.

Steve, for his part, agreed to detail their spending by category so they could discuss where the money was going and evaluate the sustainability of their spending over time. Conversations like these are vital to couples trying to navigate the uncharted waters of new wealth. Engaging in straightforward and honest dialogue, grounded in facts, helped to get Sally and Steve moving toward mutually agreed-upon goals.

Determining Financial Priorities

Often couples have difficulty agreeing on their financial priorities, and these differences of opinion can sometimes pit them against each other. James, an executive at a fast-growing, small, private business, and his wife,

Mary, had very different ideas about what the money was for. James was proud of the amount of savings he could sock away with his mid-six-figure income. Mary was grateful for their secure financial position and the luxury it afforded them, but she wanted to spend any excess money on experiences with their young family that they would remember forever. There was an innate sense of conflict in their financial priorities, as James spoke the language of savings and Mary spoke the language of experiences. Both were important and worthy goals, but prioritizing was critical for happiness in their marriage.

James handled the investments and paid most of the bills. Mary controlled the family spending at the grocery store and the kid expenses. She wasn't feeling heard when it came to scheduling family trips or talking about major purchases that would achieve the experiences she wanted for the family. James, while appreciating quality family time and enjoying travel, was focused primarily on his savings goals. He obsessed over getting the best price and minimizing costs, and his attitude toward Mary's desires was often negative because he saw her dreams as interfering with his savings targets. Basically, he didn't trust Mary to keep her spending on family experiences under control, and he tried to manage the problem with a focus on frugality. As you might imagine, this didn't produce marital harmony. Mary became resigned to the frustrating pattern of their conversations, and she stopped dreaming up opportunities for their family because it wasn't worth the inevitable fight.

I worked with James and Mary to recognize that they really wanted the same ideal outcome—fantastic family experiences at a price they could afford—and they were just coming at the problem from entrenched perspectives. They brainstormed ideas about how they could achieve their ideal outcome, and then each scored the list of ideas on a scale of 1–10 to determine their top priorities to focus on jointly. Learning to respect the value that they each brought to the family was an important part of this process: for James to appreciate the vision and passion that Mary provided in being the chief instigator for exciting ideas, and for Mary to appreciate James's detail-oriented approach to pricing out purchases and coordinating the family budget, which resulted in financial security.

They scheduled "financial dates" at Starbucks on Saturday mornings to discuss their priorities without the kids around. The goal was for James to listen to Mary, ask questions about her vision for their family's lifestyle, and understand the quality of experience she was targeting, while giving her time to lay out her expectations and hopes. There was no talk of costs or money while Mary shared her ideas. Staying in a listening posture and being curious to really understand helped James appreciate what his wife brought to the family and to their relationship. Then, and only then, would James take the ball and work out a practical application of Mary's vision, trying to get the best deal financially and organize the logistics, a skill that Mary appreciated greatly because she didn't want to take on that responsibility. After making regular financial dates a priority in their schedule, James and Mary reported back to me that they had planned a wonderful family vacation at a fabulous price, and this was going to be a model for future conversations going forward because it was so successful.

Values Alignment

Tangential to using the same language of money is understanding the values your partner holds dear. These underlying motivations drive our financial thought processes. Anthony and Brooke, a couple in their late 30s who had created wealth at Google and had significant ownership in two lifestyle-oriented private companies, were not on the same page when it came to setting a vision for their financial future.

When I met them, Anthony was not happy with their communication about money, and it caused him to be very negative when the subject came up. Brooke didn't understand why he responded this way, and so she pushed even harder to bring her ideas to fruition. That made Anthony dig his heels in even further, in an endless cycle of mutual frustration.

My first step with this couple was to review their values, and in doing so, it became clear to them and to me that there were significant differences in what they cared about. For Anthony, understanding the details, process, and research behind their financial decisions was most important, while Brooke valued exploring visionary ideas and seeing what was possible.

Anthony couldn't support her passions without having the details in place and understanding the financial impact. That made him the buzz-kill in many of their discussions. Brooke could become overcommitted to her "good ideas" and needed Anthony to slow her down at times, so they could evaluate the financial and other impacts that an idea might have on different areas of their financial and family well-being.

In working with Anthony and Brooke, my goal was to help them recognize and honor each other's values and see how those values complimented their weaknesses. Anthony was primarily interested in the practical details and the conservation of resources, while Brooke got her energy from setting big goals and aspirations and helping the family dream about what might be possible. Financial vision is important, but it also requires prudent research before taking action, while knowledge needs inspiration to bring about a future that is compelling and exciting. Both Anthony and

Brooke had a role to play, and through this newly discovered awareness of each other's values, they could both contribute to successful financial decision-making for their family.

"My Money" Versus "Our Money"

In financial conversations with couples, I often see assets accumulated prior to the beginning of the relationship—including family inheritances, earned income, and investments—creating a natural stress point related to how they view the money: "mine" versus "ours." Some couples prefer to keep their assets completely separate, while others put all the money they have into communal accounts. Still others have a combination of both—keeping most of their money as separate property, while sharing funds in jointly controlled, pooled accounts for certain expenses or savings goals.

Often, one partner in a couple is the heavy lifter when it comes to wealth creation and the other partner contributes in other ways, such as taking on the role of stay-at-home parent or working at a job they enjoy that doesn't bring in as much income. In the situation where partners are financially unbalanced—particularly when one makes all the money and the other makes none—feelings about who should make the major financial decisions and day-to-day spending decisions (who gets to spend the money, on what, and how much) can become contentious if couples do not communicate well.

There can be a tendency on the part of the main breadwinner to assume a larger voice in financial decisions. The other partner may feel judged and emotionally triggered when his or her spending isn't in line (too much or too little) with the spouse's ideas. Establishing open communication and a clear arrangement for joint, community, and separate assets is critical. [Note: There are important legal and tax considerations regarding joint, community, and separate property that are outside the scope of this book. Please consult with legal or accounting professionals to address these issues.]

Allison is the founder of a company that went from a start-up based out of her apartment to venture-backed in three short years. During this tumultuous time professionally, she was in a romantic relationship with Brett, who provided important emotional support while she worked very hard to get her company off the ground. Brett wasn't concerned at all about the financial implications for their relationship or his equity stake because his family growing up had an "all for one, one for all" approach to money within relationships. Brett was focused primarily on their long-term relationship and believed that the money would support an aligned vision for their future together. During Allison's growing-up years, she had experienced money as a tool for manipulation, and because of fear and shame attached to money, she vowed never to have money be used against her like that again. Sharing or letting others "control" her was a source of great anxiety for Allison, so keeping their modest assets segregated, in form and intent, was the only way she felt comfortable.

This arrangement left money issues quietly bubbling below the surface, until Allison's windfall from investors changed everything. There was now a large capital gain created by shares that were purchased from Allison and represented a $1 million installment against a much larger pool of wealth to come. Allison believed that wealth would calm her fears of the past, but Brett and Allison began to struggle under the stress associated with the implied ownership and practical management of the proceeds. Were they going to view the funds from an "ours" or "mine" point of view?

There was both a legal and an emotional component to the situation that needed to be addressed. Could Allison keep the assets segregated and not create relational friction for Brett? How would Brett honor Allison's worry and still trust in their long-term future together? While they were both deeply committed to the relationship, this question of "my money" versus "our money" was tearing them apart. Eventually, the couple agreed to start by addressing Allison's need for security, earmarking an initial share of funds to be invested in a pool of "safety" assets in Allison's name. Once a certain financial threshold is achieved through these investments, they will revisit the question of honoring Brett's feelings. The drama around these decisions had toxic impacts on their relationship and brought up fears and concerns that could take some time to heal.

How you communicate about the actual or implied ownership of money can create serious relational divides if not dealt with early and honestly. Even in the best of relationships, where communication is a strong suit, it can wreak havoc when money is introduced into the relational dynamic. Your money history, and specifically how your parents dealt with money, can play a huge part in how you process the accumulating wealth. Don't assume that your relationship is aligned: Hiring a wealth coach could be money well spent in these circumstances.

For wealth creators in committed relationships headed toward marriage, a prenuptial or cohabitation agreement can be used to separate assets, debt, and inherited property, and to define who gets what in the case of divorce or separation. As a senior executive at Nike shared with me, discussions around creating such a legal document to protect assets can be very emotionally triggering because you are forced to imagine, "What if the relationship doesn't work out?"

He described the experience of negotiating a prenup as "an oddity because you are spending time building a relationship, while each of you have different lawyers, and they are negotiating property ownership issues. I wasn't even sure how to think about it—it was like designing a generous parting gift ahead of time. And it brought up crazy thoughts, like 'What happens if she decides to run off with the tennis pro next week?'" In effect, you are putting boundaries around just one part of your life—your financial life—while you are breaking down barriers throughout the rest of your life in order to develop the closest relationship possible.

Despite the emotional ramifications, it is important for wealth creators to consider, "How am I protected?" when it comes to "my money" versus "our money." These agreements, whether or not they are used, have the potential to both clarify and complicate the impact of money on the relationship.

Money and Dating

For wealth creators who are single, dating and relationship decisions can be complicated by their financial status. Finding someone to date is difficult enough, but when your level of wealth is much higher than the person you are dating, many conflicts can arise. My wealth-creator clients have shared their struggles with dating: Potential dating partners are intimidated by their high-level careers. They need to know what someone does for a living and how much they make (even using the Internet to sleuth for data) before they consent to a date. They won't disclose their wealth because it creates an imbalance in the relationship. They can afford nice restaurants or expensive concert tickets, but when they pay for dates, it creates friction. "He shops at Safeway, while I shop at Whole Foods." Essentially, money can create a divide that is hard to bridge when it comes to embarking on a relationship.

Cathy, an early Microsoft employee, has found it challenging to find men to date because she is much more financially secure than most of the men she meets. For many guys, this is intimidating and emasculating, as a man's identity often is heavily wrapped up in being the provider. Cathy's fear that a relationship will really be about the money and not true love keeps her quiet on the money front.

A senior executive at a *Fortune* 100 company told me that she is virtually undatable because of her superior financial status and the perceived power imbalance this creates with the men she meets.

Another client suggests proceeding with caution until you are clear about the future of the relationship and about your own feelings and intentions. Then, once the relationship gets to a certain point, open and clear conversation is critical to establishing a relationship of trust. She also advises: "Don't try to control all the financial details and decisions, or else the other person isn't able to fully show up in the relationship. It's a difficult balance that requires patience and time."

For William, a top executive at Apple, the visibility of his current role has changed his approach to dating. He states: "I am very careful, and sensitive to the perceptions of the other person, and how they might be perceived because they are dating me. I'm very hesitant of online dating and the randomness of it so I haven't pursued that option." He worries that disparity in the financial situation of a potential dating partner would create an element of instability and distraction that he doesn't want. William feels that it's easier for men who are in his position to date successfully than it is for women in powerful, financially successful roles. He says: "Early in relationships, money usually isn't a topic of direct discussion. Many dates tend to be women from the tech industry or others who know their way around that world, and they are not intimidated by the money. People know that I am at Apple, and there is an implicit assumption that I am pretty well off." He adds that there is still fear that someone is only dating him because of his money.

William advises others who are in a similar position to go slow and ease into relationships. Ask friends to line you up with potential dating partners who will come to the relationship already vetted and knowing about your financial status and background. This can eliminate much of the concern about money and dating. Eventually, you will need to have conversations about the money, but front-load it by finding out what potential partners do to support themselves, taking time to understand their overall situation—career, background, relationship history, etc.

Like many important stages in life, it's critical to listen to and trust your gut instincts while dating. If you don't feel comfortable sharing your financial truths with a dating partner, don't. You may need some time to examine and understand your own relationship with money first (working through this book is a great first step!) Ultimately, you will need to be vulnerable in order to build intimacy with someone else. Money can sometimes feel like an impediment in establishing trust, but try to be patient with the process: Assess your comfort level at regular intervals, and test the waters by sharing small amounts of low-risk information about your finances before taking the plunge with full disclosure.

Friends and Family

It's challenging to keep money out of relationships, especially when you transition from a comfortable professional lifestyle to being independently wealthy in a short time span. Expectations change, and sometimes it's difficult to know where you stand with friends and family. True friendships require authenticity, and sometimes money can put up an artificial barrier. It can become easier to simply avoid the whole "money" topic with friends and extended family members. In fact, according to a survey conducted by Wells Fargo, 44 percent of Americans say that talking about personal finances is the toughest conversation you can have (even beating out death, which came in second at 38 percent).[37]

With friendships that begin when you are young and starting out in life, there is a sense that you're all on the same level—everyone is working hard and trying to keep up with the financial demands of daily life, starting families, etc. When one person or couple in a group suddenly shifts to a different money stratum, it can throw a wrench into those friendships. You're suddenly no longer playing on the same field. Most of the time, you can move past these challenges by continuing to be your true self in spite of the money. Occasionally, you may find yourself in a situation where, no matter how hard you try, a friend or family member can't get past your changed financial condition, and it strains or damages the relationship.

There is almost nothing you can do when a friend or family member stops seeing you for who you are and views you only through the lens of your money. This person may think of you as entitled, showy, or just a big checkbook. It's very uncomfortable to recognize this about a friend or family member, and you will likely begin to mask your own feelings when you're around this person. Eventually, you realize you can't be authentic in that relationship, and you may try to distance yourself from this person. You are left feeling misunderstood or envied without being able to clear the air or clarify whether your perceptions are correct. (Remember, we'd rather have an uncomfortable conversation about death than talk about money!) That leaves you in a really lonely and difficult place. The path of least resistance is to say nothing.

Andy and Iris were always conscientious savers, but when the stock options they held from a publicly traded healthcare company vested and were sold, it materially changed their financial status. For a while, their friends didn't have any idea that Andy and Iris had become wealthy because their day-to-day life didn't change much. They still lived in the same house, drove the same cars, and wore the same clothes, and their kids attended the same schools. But when they decided to purchase a beautiful vacation home and invited their friends to visit, they began to notice a feeling of discomfort with a few of their friends. Some were excited for them initially, but then "It must be nice" comments started to make Andy and Iris feel uncomfortable. It was jarring for them to realize that certain friendships really were changed by their new financial status. The natural impulse to share your blessings with friends can quickly become complicated.

Intimidation and Empathy

Significant financial differences between yourself and family or friends can be intimidating to those with less wealth, and it's important to understand why. Certain people may feel insecurity and embarrassment about having less material success than you. For example, perhaps your friends have a modest or small home and they want to reciprocate your generosity and entertain you. They may not feel what they have to offer is "good enough" compared to your home, resources, or lifestyle. There is sometimes a feeling that wealthy people only want to talk to other wealthy people. In some cases that stereotype can be true, or it may be a vibe given off unintentionally. Society tends to elevate wealthy people, making them seem more important or having more to offer, and that can make everyone else feel unimportant and invisible. Certainly, envy often plays a part in these feelings of difference, but many times, comments along the lines of "It must be nice to have XYZ" are really just curiosity about what the experience of wealth would be like. It may still feel hurtful when those you love act differently around you because of your money, but it helps to understand where they are coming from.

To keep friendships and family relationships around money healthy, be empathetic toward those with fewer resources and remember how you have felt when in that position. Show genuine interest in their lives regardless of financial circumstances, and cut them some slack when it feels like they might be experiencing a visit from the green monster. In addition, don't become cavalier about your freedom from money worries and make insensitive comments about money that could damage the relationship. For example, keep yourself from saying things like: "It's just $50 to do x or y." It might not seem like a big deal to you, but that may not be the case for your friends or family members.

Birds of a Feather

One of the risks of only hanging out with people with similar financial means is that you can lose touch with the financial reality of how other people live. When you say things that might make a less financially secure friend feel "less than," even innocently, it can lead people to avoid relationships with you.

The biggest difference between first-generation wealth and second- or third-generation wealth is that you have relationships with people who can relate to your circumstances. Wealth can be like a force of gravity that pulls you into orbit with other people who have the same financial dynamics as you. Even though there are focused attempts not to change old friendships, new friends are often wealthier or in a similar financial position to you because of the things, places, and experiences that tend to attract people with money.

It can be a self-selecting process of sorts toward people with a similar financial situation. Harry, a senior executive with a fast-growing biotech firm, recently shared that a family trip to the Sundance Film Festival was a poignant confirmation of that statement. Most of his friends couldn't afford this type of trip, and he ended up developing close friendships with some people they met at the festival who attend this type of event regularly. That's how the winnowing process subtly happens: You flock to friends who relate to your situation and can afford to do the same things you want to do.

Keeping Quiet

It seems obvious why some of you might be thinking about keeping your wealth discreet and trying to blend in instead of standing out. I find that to be the case in Seattle where I live, where it's commonplace to be understated about your wealth. One client in particular bragged to me that he is still driving his 15-year-old Honda to work and has all his old friendships intact—evidence I guess that he is the same person before and after the money arrived. The more common outcome is to hear complaints about the difficulty of making close friends. Keeping your wealth a secret limits the level of vulnerability about your life, but simultaneously limits the depth of your relationships.

A couple who unexpectedly received a large distribution from a family business recently told me that the circle of friends with whom they could share their struggles was nonexistent. They said: "We haven't been intentional about seeking out relationships with people who are dealing with the same problems we are because we thought we might be the only ones with the problem, and maybe there is something wrong with us."

There can be just as much discomfort and shame about having money as there is with not having money. You may feel that you are the only one experiencing issues with wealth and worry how you might come off if you complain about the ways that your life has changed because of the money.

Rick, a software developer and wealth beneficiary from a major gaming company, hasn't shared his financial success with any of his friends or family. He is extremely afraid of the relational ramifications his money may cause. However, there is a lot of stress in keeping such an important part of your life a secret and worrying about being found out. Rick doesn't want to be viewed as a big checkbook by his friends and doesn't want to wonder if they only like him for his money.

Paying for Things

Sometimes being the only one in your friend or family circle who has financial resources can lead to feelings of aloneness—you're the only one who can afford a special trip or other experience that you really want to have. So you end up paying for others to join you. It can exacerbate the relational awkwardness to pay for everything when you are out with friends and family unless this has been discussed in advance and agreed upon.

There can be a genuine desire to treat everyone to exquisite meals and extravagant experiences out of your financial abundance because it feels good to give, especially to the people you care most about. Generosity is a wonderful trait; however, allowing others to also contribute is important too. Consider modifying your approach: Adapt the level of restaurant or experience to allow your friends and family to contribute if they choose, rather than selecting restaurants or travel experiences that are well beyond their financial means.

This doesn't mean you shouldn't use your money to pay for amazing experiences and invite your friends along. It feels really good to take care of others with your money. Taking a few girlfriends to the spa or picking up the tab on a vacation rental will likely be appreciated by your friends and family, but sometimes this can be triggering to people with less money. Have an intentional conversation about what you would like to contribute, and discuss how they might also contribute somewhere along the way. Talking about money with friends and extended family members can feel awkward at first, but establishing open communication about your genuine desire to share your wealth can pave the way to healthier relationships down the road.

A couple I've worked with addresses the issue of paying for things by first examining each of their friendships as a unique situation. They try to be particularly sensitive to differences in financial means, and they've made it a priority to maintain their friendships with a broad cross section of people from different economic strata. With friends who don't have their financial means, they might suggest hitting some food trucks for takeout and going back to their house for a game night, rather than dinner at an expensive restaurant and taking in a Broadway show. By keeping expectations for activities at an appropriate financial level, they've continued to enjoy valued relationships.

Financial Support for Family and Friends

The reverse of this situation is when family and friends expect you to grab for the check every time because you have the most money. Sometimes wealth creators assume that others expect them to cover expenses, and this is uncomfortable. There is often a fear that the only reason some people spend time with you is because they seek to profit from the relationship, hoping to do business with you or have you invest in their ideas. Some friends and family members may straight up expect you to share your wealth with them.

Unfortunately, money can bring out the worst in some people. While this can be extremely frustrating if it happens all the time, err on the side of patience. Again, having conversations about financial expectations may be the solution to getting everyone on the same page about what you plan to pay for and what you do not. Sadly, some relationships become simply too difficult to maintain because of expectations around money or jealousy, and several of my clients have mentioned losing friendships over issues connected to their wealth.

Naturally, there are concerns about giving large amounts of money to family and friends who might not have any experience managing it wisely and who may squander it. We've all heard stories about bad outcomes such as money being used for drugs, or paying down credit card debt only to have the friend or relative back in debt and asking for more several years later. It can make you feel used and certainly discourage you from offering future financial help if such behavior continues. It can also strain your family and friend relationships if you don't provide financial help when asked.

Because money is such an emotional subject for people, the outcomes of financial dealings with friends and family can create long-term impacts. If you do give money to those who ask, there may be bad outcomes, and if you don't give, there can be resentments that last for many years. If you decide to lend money to friends or family, take the position that if the loan isn't paid back, you will still value the relationship, or don't make the loan. In fact, a loan is probably better thought of as a gift.

I believe it's important to use your values as the framework to make wise decisions about helping out family and friends with your wealth. For example, if education is important to you, then consider helping your siblings pay for education expenses for your nieces and nephews, at a level you feel comfortable with. If friendship and experiences are top values, invite close friends to join you on an all-expenses-paid adventure vacation. Or perhaps you might open and fund retirement accounts for family members, where your values of security and freedom can be expressed in providing loved ones a comfortable future.

My client Kathy highly valued health and wellness in her life, and she spent liberally on her own health, from spa visits to trainers, organic food, and nutrition. Her parents were experiencing health issues but couldn't afford the kind of wellness benefits that she enjoyed. Kathy was inspired to give them the gift of health, covering her father's medical needs and splurging on naturopathic doctors, massage, supplements, and healthier food. Her generosity emerged from a value she cared deeply about, which made gifting even more rewarding for Kathy. When the money you spend on family and friends aligns with your values, you're much more likely to be satisfied with the outcome of your generosity.

My wife and I value courage, adventure, and serving others less fortunate. We had the opportunity to put our money where our values are when our daughter came to us after her high school graduation with an unexpected request. She wanted to postpone college for a gap year working with a nonprofit called Youth with a Mission in Cambodia and Thailand, caring for young women trapped in sex trafficking. While this wasn't how we thought our financial support for our daughter would materialize, we quickly realized that she was embracing an important part of her life story that aligned well with the values we hold dear. With the benefit of hindsight, we can now see how our financial decision to support her completely changed the trajectory of her life, as she eventually decided to pursue a career in social work.

In general, my advice is to enjoy the freedom that comes with not having to worry about every last penny, and try not to let it change who you are, what you care about, or how you show that to those you love. There may be a few relationships you lose on the margins, but staying true to yourself and understanding the potential pain points will help keep your relationships healthy.

CONSIDER YOUR RELATIONSHIPS AND ANSWER THE FOLLOWING QUESTIONS FOR YOURSELF:

- How is money affecting your relationships positively? Negatively?
- What rating would you give to your communication level around money with your spouse or partner? (1 = poor, 10 = excellent) What is one positive step

you could take to improve communication about money with your spouse or partner?

- What is your fondest hope for your money and your family and friendships?
- What do you wish your close family and friends knew about your money or financial life that you keep secret?

CHAPTER SIX

Money and Your Kids

Wealth creators can afford to give their children tremendous advantages, in terms of education, experiences, and luxuries, but affluence also creates special issues for kids. Raising financially competent, emotionally healthy kids is a big concern for wealth creators. In this chapter, we will discuss ideas for actively teaching financial literacy, setting financial expectations and consequences, and the importance of generosity in building empathy. Most important, wealth creators can help their children have a healthier relationship with money by decoupling wealth from success. We'll explore the tools and techniques that parents can use to help their children avoid common negative impacts of growing up wealthy, including lifelong financial dependency, destructive values about money, loss of hard-earned family wealth through financial mismanagement, conflict and resentments about money, and lack of incentive to live a life of substance and meaning.

Robert Kenny, a developmental psychologist and senior advisor at the Center on Wealth and Philanthropy at Boston College, led a research project in 2012 delving into the thoughts, attitudes, and aspirations of high-wealth individuals. His findings revealed that wealthy parents are concerned about the effect that money will have on their children, including "the way their children would be treated by others and stereotyped as rich kids or trust fund babies, they wondered if their children would know if people really loved them or their money, whether they'd know if their achievements were because of their own skills, knowledge, and talent or because they have a lot of money. . . . They worried that if their children have enough money and don't have to worry about covering the mortgage, what will motivate them? How will they lead meaningful lives? This is where the money might get in the way and make things confusing, not necessarily better."[38]

I have found that issues surrounding kids and money are a big concern for the wealth creators I work with. In a series of interviews conducted with my clients recently, imparting strong money values to their children was at the top of the list of concerns for over half of my respondents. "I have big concerns about my kids growing up under this financial bubble," remarked one interviewee. "I'm very sensitive to the problem of raising my kids as entitled," added another.

Affluent children have tremendous advantages, but they often lack basic life skills that many of their nonaffluent peers acquire early in life. Kids without as many resources are forced to do a lot more for themselves at a young age, make tough choices, work harder, and deal with real consequences. Wealth creators have the luxury of providing their kids with a virtually pain-free childhood, which unfortunately comes with a downside.

Dan Baker, in his book *What Happy People Know*, sums up an issue that affluent parents and children have to deal with: "The human mind, body, and spirit thrive on struggle and challenge, just as a muscle thrives on exercise. Satisfaction without effort . . . creates only dissipation, alienation, boredom, weakness, and a sense of worthlessness."[39] Identity issues, lack of motivation, embarrassment, and isolation are common by-products of affluence affecting adults and children alike. Kids in particular are prone to experience satisfaction without effort, as parents with the best of intentions provide for their every need and want.

The good news is there are plenty of things you can do to mitigate the effects of affluence and help your kids develop a healthy relationship with money.

Talking to Your Kids About Money

"Hey, Dad, how much is your company worth?"

I could feel the tension rising in my body as I tried to act like my daughter's question wasn't a big deal. I slowly continued clearing dishes off the table while deciding how to maneuver around this potential minefield. "Well, your mother and I feel really blessed to have started a company that provides us with a nice house in a nice neighborhood, allows us do some wonderful things as a family, and is worth something. It's amazing, actually."

"Is it worth more than $1 million?" Waiting for a reaction from me. "$2 million?"

"Maybe. Maybe more. The amount isn't really that important, is it?"

"So, your company is worth more than $2 million? Wow!"

"Wait, I didn't say that!"

As parents, we often don't know how to talk to our kids about money. Even I find it tough—and for the past 25 years, I've been guiding and stewarding the wealth and aspirations of some of the most successful wealth creators in the country. Whether they become wealthy slowly or suddenly, one of the biggest concerns that clients share with me, after the need to protect their wealth, is the impact that this money will have on their kids. "How do I keep them motivated and prevent them from becoming materialistic or entitled?" is a common question.

The first step in helping your kids have a healthy relationship with money is communication. Your relationship with money will have a natural follow-on effect on your kids—they will take their cues about what money means, its purpose, and its power from you. Open, continual dialogue about earning, spending, saving, investing, and giving will prepare your children to have a high money EQ as adults.

Determining how much to share about your finances with your kids and when to do so can be a tough call. My advice: Be transparent about your wealth. Many high-wealth parents put off having conversations about money. A 2012 study conducted by U.S. Trust found that "more than half of high-net-worth boomer parents had not fully disclosed their wealth to their offspring, while another 13 percent kept completely mum."[40] This lack of transparency creates kids who aren't prepared for the wealth that will one day be coming their way.

Parents should talk to their kids about family values and beliefs around money during their formative years—in an age-appropriate way. Frugality, budgets, saving, generosity, use of debt, and entrepreneurialism are all examples of money values that can be discussed and modeled in various age-appropriate ways.

One of my clients created a family mission statement based on their values, which became a focal point for talking with their children. Philanthropy was a key focus for this family, so we helped them create a pie chart showing the distribution of their charitable giving among causes they cared about, including education, church, environment, and social issues. My clients used this visual representation to help their children understand how to put values and words into meaningful action.

Modeling prudent financial choices as a parent is the first step toward teaching your children the value of frugality and sticking to a budget, although there is no guarantee that your kids will choose to follow your lead. Often, parents find that some of their children are innately cautious with money, while others seem to spend thoughtlessly. One client recently shared with me their family strategy for two children who had very different responses to the allowance system they put into place. Their daughter embraced the family value of frugality and had no problem with the allowance they provided. She spent her money carefully on her needs and wants and made it a priority to save as well. Unfortunately, their teenage son saw the allowance as an annuity stream with no end. He was constantly out of money and asking for more, which was the opposite of the lesson they were trying to teach about living within your means.

They pivoted and helped their son formulate an appropriate budget for his high school needs, and then capped this budget as all the money he would receive for those items during the year. They were amazed by the about-face he did: Suddenly, he was very conscious of his expenses and what he was spending money on. He cut his spending and began accumulating excess funds, which he decided to invest in buying a few stocks. Through this experience, he discovered a real passion for investing and learned a great life lesson about budgeting.

The Gift of a Financial Education

Deliberate discussions about your values and the responsibilities associated with wealth, behavior modeling, and ultimately transparency about your wealth are critical to helping kids understand, appreciate, and successfully manage money. Learning wise money management can and should begin when kids are younger, not when they are about to leave the nest. In fact, whenever parents interact with money or make financial decisions, they are modeling attitudes, values, and behaviors that children are quick to pick up on.

Kids must be carefully taught basic life skills, like how to clean a bathroom or check the oil in their car, and learning how to manage their money is no different. Often, what they have learned about money is "Ask and ye shall receive." As you can probably guess, this bit of wisdom doesn't lead to financial independence. In fact, you may find that it's really challenging to instill certain values around money when there's lots of it around.

Many of my clients are first-generation wealth creators. Because they did not grow up with wealth, they feel like they are "charting new territory" as they try to raise their kids to have strong values around money in a culture that emphasizes overconsumption. There are particular obstacles for affluent families when it comes to building financial competence.

My friend Seth has struggled with these issues while raising his two sons, ages 10 and 13, within the wealth bubble of Seattle. Seth's experience growing up was very different than that of his children. With two schoolteacher parents, money was scarce in his home, and Seth learned quickly that if he wanted anything beyond the basics, he would have to earn the money for it himself. That he did: He had a paper route, mowed lawns, and did other odd jobs to earn money in his early teens; worked as a dishwasher 20 hours a week throughout high school; and supported himself through college working on the school's grounds crew and as a bank teller.

Seth says: "When money is abundant, kids can have difficulty understanding that it's a limited resource and may have no idea about the effort it takes to earn it. It's also easy for parents to fix problems or overly indulge when there isn't a financial constraint. I made this mistake when my son broke his iPod and was distraught. I replaced it, he didn't experience any pain, and I lost a powerful teaching moment. If he had to earn the money to replace it, I'm sure he would have quickly learned to take better care of his things. Similarly, there really isn't that much left for them to want when we have so much stuff. I also worry that while my standard of living continued to increase after I left the nest, they may experience a marked decline, which may lead them to live outside their means."

Seth has started to be more deliberate in teaching his children about the value of money by making a few simple changes, such as imposing natural consequences—if something breaks, it isn't automatically replaced. Kids have to earn the money to get it fixed or buy a replacement. Rather than buying a lot of big-ticket presents for Christmas or birthdays, Seth has deliberately chosen to reduce the amount of stuff in his boys' lives. If they want an Xbox, they can work and save for it. They have a list of jobs they can do around the house, with a price set for each chore.

The goal of financial education is to raise financially responsible adults with positive values about money and useful financial skills. Financial training and education should begin as soon as children are old enough for pocket money (around kindergarten or first grade). A good financial education can provide a wonderful foundation for your child as she or he learns to manage wealth on his own. Here are some practical ideas you may want to apply with your kids:

Allowances give children the opportunity to budget and make mistakes.

For younger children, a small weekly allowance is a great way to begin teaching about spending, saving for things that they want and need, and responsibility. Instead of buying your children the treats they want, teach them that they can bring their own money to the store, that they can only buy something within their budget, explain how sales tax works, and let them handle the cash transaction, counting out dollars and cents.

As your kids hit the teen years, give them expenses to manage on their own, with an allowance that is large enough to cover their needs but small enough to force them to compromise. For example, you might give them $500 per month to cover school lunches, entertainment, hobbies, trips to Starbucks, a cell phone, clothes, transportation, savings, and charity. If your children start making their lunch, downgrade their data plans, and skip Starbucks so they can save more toward a goal, congratulations—they have figured out budgeting!

Show children the family's expenses.

Consider sharing your family budget (or part of it) with your kids. For younger children, it can be helpful to get out the Monopoly play money and hand them a "salary" in paper bills, along with a list of expenses. Let them "pay the bills" and see in concrete terms where all the money goes. It's also important to let your kids see what their portion of the expenses is.

Talk through financial decisions with the kids, explaining the trade-offs you make when you choose to spend money on one thing versus another. This is a great opportunity to identify together what expenses are needs versus wants. Show them how you decide to make substantial purchases, shop for the best products and prices, and decide what you can afford. Be sure to provide examples of decisions that include delaying or denying purchases.

Establish a checking/savings account with a debit card to give hands-on experience with money.

A savings account is a great start for younger kids, and being able to check their growing balance regularly can incentivize saving part of their weekly allowance for longer-term financial goals. For teens, having their own checking account makes the budgeting exercise feel more real and holds them accountable to someone other than their parents (i.e., the bank). There's nothing like an insufficient funds fee to get their attention! When they have mastered this, consider helping older teens sign up for a credit card so they can establish a credit history. Keep in mind this can have consequences to credit scores (yours and theirs) if bungled, so you may want to do some hand-holding at first and set up an accountability system.

Set up consequences and make agreements.

Inevitably, your children will make a financial mistake: a bad purchase, spending more than they have, or missing a bill. For low-stakes mistakes (your 11-year-old spent her entire allowance on a toy and now doesn't have enough cash to go to a movie with a friend), let them experience the pain of natural consequences. It's much better for them to feel a little pain now and learn an important lesson about wise money management.

For older kids, where the stakes can be a lot higher, you will have to decide whether to bail them out or allow them to suffer the consequences of their mistake. Establishing a clear agreement with your children upfront about what they are responsible for and what you are responsible for when it comes to money is important—otherwise, they can blame you when things go wrong. Consider leaving some high-stakes responsibilities out of your teenager's hands. For example, it might sound like a good idea for kids to pay their own auto insurance, but the risk of missing a payment might be too high.

Teach them to invest.

This is a great opportunity to get kids thinking about money from a long-term perspective. For younger kids, you might give them a couple hundred dollars and work together to choose one or two stocks to invest in. Then teach them how to track the daily ups and downs of their investment on the stock market. It's a great way to begin understanding how investments work.

Some parents give their kids a "starter package" of investments to be used for long-term goals, like a down payment for a home or helping to fund a business idea. The investment will have more meaning and purpose if they have already have a vision of what the money will be used for in the future.

Foster a stewardship mindset.

Money is a tool, not a toy. Teaching kids to be stewards of family wealth helps them to see beyond the material things they can obtain with money and to understand the power of money to effect change in the world. Build a generosity muscle through acts of service or volunteering, and you'll personally reap the dual benefits of making the world a better place and enjoying the feel-good effects of giving.

Include your children in your philanthropic and volunteer efforts and they will gain perspective on their own good fortune, as well as positive reinforcement for giving versus getting. Being a good steward of wealth also requires financial management skills like budgeting, which acknowledges the reality that neither time nor money is a limitless resource.

Kids and Work

Sigmund Freud famously said, "Love and work are the cornerstones of our humanness." At its core, work gives us a sense of being useful in the world. Giving kids opportunities to experience the satisfaction that comes from working hard can start when they are quite young. Begin teaching your children about work by requiring them to participate in a "job" at whatever level is appropriate for their age, whether that is chores at home for younger children or a paying job for older kids.

Consider keeping a list of chores to do around the house, and let friends and relatives know that your kids are available to work. This can be a good step toward eventually getting a real, part-time job. Keep in mind that they may want to work only if there is something they want to buy, so do your best to keep them wanting.

Parents often say that they don't want their teens to have a part-time job because school, sports, and extracurricular activities are already stressing their kids out, and they fear that letting their kids work will put them at a disadvantage academically compared to kids who don't. However, work provides a sense of competence and satisfaction that sports and school do not. A summer job may be the best compromise for teens who don't have the time or inclination to work during the school year.

Before Warren Buffett became the Oracle of Omaha, he delivered newspapers. Oprah Winfrey worked at a grocery store; Colin Powell, a furniture store. The author Stephen King worked as a janitor. George Clooney sold shoes. The lowly summer job is part of the biography of many successful people: proof that they started with no special advantages, understood the value of hard work, and succeeded because of their effort and ingenuity, not because of family wealth or special favors.

These are lessons that we universally value. If money is not really an issue, are the lessons learned from having a job more valuable than the lessons learned from participating in sports, or mastering a musical instrument? Is having a job more important than the bonding that occurs during a family vacation? Should our children spend their time out of school earning minimum wage, or studying and preparing for college? These are all questions that you and your children should carefully consider when it comes to teens and work.

Wealth creators have a passion for hard work and respect the rewards that work can bring. They want to impart these same values to their children, while also giving them the means to pursue their dreams. They want to give their children opportunities to learn, without creating hardships that might hold them back. In my experience, a parent's desire to protect and support their children sometimes is at odds with their desire to prepare them for the real world. It really doesn't matter if the work is menial and the pay is low—a summer job provides teens with experience far beyond the work itself. This is a good time for them to learn about writing résumés, interviewing for a job, starting a savings account, and paying taxes.

Helping kids understand the importance of work and directing them on a path toward meaningful, useful employment is critical to their long-term happiness, and yours. Particularly if Mom and Dad have retired young and aren't modeling a more "normal" working life, kids may be confused about what their own career trajectory should look like. Your kids should know that they are expected to work, both to earn money to support themselves and to find purpose and enjoyment in using their gifts and talents.

Kids also need to see Mom and Dad working (whether that work is compensated or volunteer), because as any parent of teenagers knows, actions speak louder than words. Pursue meaningful vocations in your own life that align with your core values, talents, and interests and that allow you to make a unique contribution to the world. Share stories and insights with your children about the work you do and have done in the past—both the jobs you enjoyed and the ones you didn't—and what you learned from those experiences.

Try using a "Visioning Exercise" with your teens. Catching a vision of what their adult life might look like can provide motivation and guidance as they make important decisions about college and courses of study. Help them explore different careers and what they pay, drawing the connection between career choice and lifestyle. Get them talking about what kind of material possessions are important to them, where and how they want to live, and the impact they wish to make on the world. This is also a great time to remind them that saving money when they are young makes much more of an impact than starting when they're older.

Ask your kids about the future they want to achieve. Try asking them these questions:

- What do you dream about doing or being in your life?
- How do you define success in life, work, money?
- What are you afraid of or worrying about in life, work, money?
- What subjects, activities, hobbies make you feel most alive? Joyful? Happy?

When helping children envision future careers and lifestyles, it is easy to conflate success with money. Instead, help them define success for themselves. Explain that success means different things to different people, and that cultural norms of success can lure them down a dangerous and unfulfilling path. Help them to understand your family values and your definition of success. (You might refer to Chapter One for ideas on redefining success for yourself, and Chapter Seven for help in defining your core values.)

Having these conversations regularly can empower your child's decision-making and steer them toward satisfying educational and career goals.

Financial Support and Setting Expectations

Preventing your children from becoming financially dependent requires clarity and intentional communication about your financial contribution to their success and their own responsibility for the outcome. I know from my experience as a parent that it is very difficult to see my children struggle or even fail without wanting to jump in and fix it. The key is establishing clear financial boundaries and limiting the safety net before emotions run high. An unlimited financial safety net can stifle a child's ability to build character and self-confidence while learning important life lessons by overcoming difficult situations. Your emotional support can be limitless, but your financial support should not.

Launching their children well is one of the biggest worries for high-wealth parents: They fear that their own success will negatively influence their children's ambitions. They're right to be worried. According to the Williams Group wealth consultancy, 70 percent of wealthy families lose their wealth by the second generation, and 90 percent by the third.[41] The fact is, children don't profit from being handed everything they want. If they don't have to work for it, they likely won't.

Warren Buffett told *Fortune* magazine that he plans to leave his kids "enough money so that they would feel they could do anything, but not so much that they could do nothing."[42] When asked how much of his vast fortune he will leave his children, Bill Gates once said they will have their educations paid for, but beyond that, they will not receive very much. He said that he expects his children to find their passion and work hard.

As kids get older, clearly communicate expectations about the amount of financial support you will give them as they grow up. Be specific: You might be willing to cover a used car (but not a new one), or college expenses (but not graduate school). Perhaps you plan to give them a down payment for their first home. How long will you offer support? Until age 25? Age 35? Do your kids have to meet certain expectations in order to receive your financial support, such as maintaining a certain grade point average (GPA) to have their college expenses paid for? Some of these decisions might feel arbitrary if you have the means to help a lot.

Start by getting a clear vision of the future lifestyle you desire for your kids. I'm often surprised at how little parents have thought about this question. The lifestyle that your kids enjoy now is based on *your* financial success and may not be the lifestyle that they are able to achieve when they leave the nest. They need to be prepared for what could be a big change as they head out on their own. The author Cyril Northcote Parkinson wrote, "A luxury, once enjoyed, becomes a necessity."[43] Once you are accustomed to a certain lifestyle, it is really hard to go back. The more grounded your lifestyle is, the less of a leap your kids have to make when they leave the nest.

Children grow up with unique interests, passions, and life stories, even though they are raised in the same household and with the same parenting style as their siblings. There are distinct differences in each of our three kids, and differences in the kind of support that they each needed as we raised them. All parents face decisions about how to use their resources to support their children as they develop and grow into adults. If you have more than one child, these decisions become even more complicated.

Do you adopt a policy of "fair and equitable," where each child will essentially be treated the same financially in terms of paying for camps, sports, hobbies, and education opportunities? Or is there a filter that applies appropriate financial support for the circumstances? If one child is gifted academically or athletically and doesn't need her or his college expenses to be paid thanks to scholarships, does she or he receive the same funds that a sibling would have been given for college expenses, to provide for other needs like a first home, car, etc.? If one child chooses a career that will provide abundant financial resources and your other child chooses to be a teacher or social worker, will you step in and provide assistance for the one who doesn't make as much money? When one child is extremely self-sufficient financially and others always seem to be in need, how do you keep things fair and equitable among your children?

Business owners Peter and Sally were facing these decisions with their three children. Two of them had strong careers and were doing fine financially. Their younger daughter was recently divorced, raising a child with disabilities and still earning her degree. Peter and Sally decided to offer a fair and equitable level of support but to use a needs-based timing approach that looks at each child's individual circumstances.

This means that they are providing a house for their daughter right now, as well as other financial support to help with childcare needs. They plan to gift a similar dollar amount of equity to their other daughter, who is working in the family business. They communicated their intention to provide their son with equivalent support when the need arises.

They have worked hard to be very sensitive to the emotional impact of this generosity on their children. Peter and Sally approached the situation with a long-term outlook: They consider those funds as an advance on their daughter's future inheritance, and they will make the necessary adjustments in their estate planning to make sure their other kids are treated fairly as this approach evolves over the years.

It's common to hear from wealth creators that one of their children "gets it," and by that, they mean budgeting, investing, and using money wisely. They are often worried about another of their children, who has tendencies to either be oblivious to money or indulge in reckless splurges and a taste for the finer things. It can be stressful for parents to know what to do in these circumstances, especially because they tend to feel better about providing financial support for a more responsible child.

It's best to exercise caution and go slow when it comes to making decisions involving downstream impacts for different children, if your inclination is to entrust fewer resources to a less financially mature child. Unequal financial support between siblings is usually a recipe for bigger problems down the road. Using natural consequences and honest conversation to teach financial discipline (as noted previously) can be the best salve in these challenging moments.

Inheritance: Who Gets My Money?

It's a topic that no one likes to think about: What will happen to my kids when I'm gone? For wealth creators, it is particularly important to carefully consider the outcomes you want for your children after your death. If you have kids and don't have a will yet, it's a good idea to begin some estate planning. You may also find trust vehicles to be useful, and I discuss them in this section.

Perhaps you haven't given much thought yet to who will inherit your growing estate. This very important tactical decision can force a potentially challenging conversation to the surface—namely, how much are you planning to give to your family, including kids if you have them. Discussing this may seem surreal and not very fun to think about, probably because you are still vibrant, healthy, and young, but putting a stake in the ground on these decisions will help give you peace of mind for your family's future.

Communication is key when it comes to leaving a legacy for your children and grandchildren. Researchers at the Williams Group surveyed more than 2,000 affluent families over 20 years and found that "60 percent of the time, a trust and communication breakdown among family members played the biggest role" in the deterioration of inherited family wealth. The same study reported that "another 25 percent of the time, the banana peel turned out to be the families' failure to prepare heirs for their pending prosperity. . . . many heirs are kept deliberately in the dark about their financial good fortune until the day Mom and Dad drop the trust-fund bomb and shove a stack of legal papers in front of them to sign."[44] Ill-prepared children coming into windfalls equals downfall.

Given all the developmental implications of wealth and the many examples of money wreaking havoc on the lives of young people who inherit significant sums, you may feel slightly panicked about the reality of your kids getting all that money after you're gone. Remember, your other choices are to leave it to other family members, friends, and/or charities, and to give some of it to the government via taxes, so there are options. The ultimate decision is very personal, and solutions vary from transferring as much wealth to the kids as possible to giving them a set amount (such as $2–5 million), with the balance going to other beneficiaries and charity.

There are several things that will materially influence the inheritance decision: the size and composition of your net worth and the current age of your children. If children are very young or teenagers, and even young twentysomethings, there can be a lot of angst about how much to give them because you don't have a full perspective yet on how they will launch into adulthood.

In this situation, it's common for parents to set up trust distribution mechanisms that are triggered by reaching a certain age. For example, $1 million inheritance at age 35, $1 million at age 45, and $1 million at age 55, if the total inheritance goal was $3 million. (Some of you may be beneficiaries of an estate plan set up by your parents that uses similar age-based distributions.) In other cases, trusts can be established to distribute regular income streams, as well as for specific purposes such as business start-up expenses, home down payment, and education costs, and even to benefit future generations. There are a variety of strategies available to wealth creators based on their objectives, and it is important to seek the advice of a competent attorney at this stage.

When it comes to estate planning, the starting point for almost everyone is to keep the inheritance equal among all the children, limiting potential future friction. The number of future grandchildren will add additional complexity to the mix, as we'll discuss in a moment. In other more complex asset scenarios involving real estate, it's common to see families making a distinction between liquid assets, which may be capped at a certain amount for each child, and the family home and vacation properties, which often have sentimental value and are gifted to all the children to control and enjoy together, along with operating reserves for property taxes and maintenance.

A variety of other situations create opportunities to customize and make adjustments from the starting point of an equitable base for each child, including the education of grandchildren, special needs, financial hardship, and business-owning families. You may opt to pay for college or private school for your grandchildren through your estate, with the result that your child who has a greater number of children will get more money than one with fewer or no children.

The other place I often see customization is when parents provide additional financial support for an adult child who is struggling or in a lower-paying career than the other siblings. The key to making that work is being clear with each family member about what is going on and why. There doesn't need to be agreement, but if you aren't open about your plans and reasons for those plans (which is often the case), it can create a relational mess.

When parents change the distribution of their estate to inequitably favor a more financially needy adult child, other siblings who are working hard and haven't received as much ongoing financial assistance from parents can feel upset and harbor resentment. I've seen this go both ways: In one case, a successful wealth creator was happy to disclaim any future inheritance from his parents in favor of his brother, who needed it much more. Another client was deeply wounded by her parents' decision, and lingering feelings of being treated unfairly have left persistent emotional scars.

In business-owning families, issues arise over how to gift to kids employed in the business versus those not in the business. Often, shares are given to the kids in the business and the real estate related to the business is gifted to the other kids. Over time, valuation gaps can be created because the business may appreciate much faster than the real estate. Those who inherit the real estate can become frustrated and feel mistreated because they feel that they got a bad deal. Giving shares equally to everyone, whether they work in the business or not, creates potential stressors about how to invest or spend the profits. In addition, shares in each family can get unintentionally diluted based on the number of grandchildren in each family, leading to a concern about future power struggles for control over the business.

Like many things in life, age-appropriate communication is the key to avoiding the many pitfalls and dynamics at play when it comes to transferring assets to your children. When possible, be open about your estate planning so that expectations are shared ahead of time, whether the distribution plan is equal or not. As you might imagine, this simple step can go much further to keep harmony among your heirs than any grand strategy devised by a wealth manager and attorney.

If inheritance isn't talked about until after your death, you risk significant family disruptions, bad feelings, and misunderstandings. Inherited money can build up and tear down relationships, and it's important to understand the critical elements that allow the transfer of your financial wealth in a way that helps future generations to flourish.

The Truth About Trusts

For tax and estate-planning reasons, many wealthy parents set up trust accounts for their kids. If your children have money set aside, it is essential to prepare them for what's coming. Don't let a significant distribution of money become a major distraction in their 20s or beyond. Teaching children to be good stewards, what money means and doesn't mean, and the purpose of the funds gives them a framework for managing the responsibility well.

When considering various estate and tax-planning strategies that involve giving irrevocable gifts to children or grandchildren through trusts, please think through the potential downstream effects and implications. I've seen trust documents that were designed with the best intentions by Grandma and Grandpa cause major strife within families because distribution language and rules did not adequately address the family dynamics that developed decades after they were created. These instruments can exist for a long time, and it's important to plan ahead for that fact.

The other issue occurs when the intent is to manipulate and control beneficiary behavior through the trust, either during your lifetime or after death. This is referred to as "dead hand control."

The people who are most disappointed with the results created by trusts are usually those who set them up in a hurry to save taxes due to an initial public offering (IPO) or a liquidity transaction on the near horizon. In such situations, 100 percent of the thought goes into tax planning and 0 percent on how the trust may impact family dynamics or the beneficiaries' lives.

For example, when parents create irrevocable trusts for young children to save taxes, they can't know what the future holds for their kids. You may end up with a trust that is overly generous with distributions to a child who is struggling and financially irresponsible, or a trust that is too restrictive for a kid who grows into a very responsible young adult. In many cases, it is better to wait until children have matured so the trusts can be appropriately customized to their needs (even though it isn't as tax effective to wait).

Please keep in mind that trusts are not an effective tool to correct undesirable behavior patterns in your children. If your kids have never experienced financial consequences in childhood, it's going to be tough for them to accept limitations and consequences when a trustee enforces strict distribution rules.

Often, parents try to make the trust very restrictive because they are worried that the trust will reduce a young adult's incentive to work hard, which is a valid concern. However, if the child was raised in an environment where the family always flew first class, ate at the finest restaurants, drove fancy cars, and lived in luxury, it is a form of cruelty to suddenly cut them off and make trust distributions very difficult to get. Yes, they can learn to survive on modest income or distributions, but it can also cause major resentments and family strife.

Parents can do all the right things with their children in terms of setting expectations and creating a thoughtful trust, only to find out later that the children really want to make it on their own and don't want the safety net. Sometimes parents will try to incentivize trusts by paying a distribution equal to whatever each child earns, or what each one earns up to a certain amount.

The problem with this plan is you can have one child who is a teacher trying to get by on $50,000 and another working as an executive who makes $300,000. That means that the teacher would get a $50,000 distribution from the trust, while the executive would get $300,000. Not fair, right? In general, it's best to keep things as equal as possible among siblings and not try to get too fancy or controlling with trusts.

It's important for parents to realize that while providing financial security for their kids seems to make sense and their intentions are good, trusts can still backfire. Thus, waiting until kids are older and asking them how you can invest in them can be far more effective than funding trusts earlier than you need to, often to save taxes.

Money conversations are often awkward and complicated, even (maybe especially) with our kids. But putting them off—or never having them at all—isn't the answer. Having open, age-appropriate conversations with our children about money is the best way to set them on a path to a fulfilling and secure future.

This includes discussing realistic financial expectations, from childhood allowances to teen budgeting, college expenses, and launching into independent adult life, trusts, and inheritances. Helping our children understand the responsibilities of wealth stewardship and keep the "long game" in mind is serious business, and one that can start now, regardless of what your net worth is today.

CONSIDER YOUR CHILDREN AND THE INFLUENCE OF MONEY ON THE RELATIONSHIP AS YOU ANSWER THE FOLLOWING QUESTIONS:

- What lessons from your money story might you share with your children? Remember, both good and bad choices and experiences can make great teaching tools.

- What does "launching your children well" mean to you from a financial perspective? What does your ideal outcome look like?

- How can you use your values to teach your children creatively about money management?

- Considering their unique needs, how are you planning to provide financial support for each of your children? Equally? Based on need and circumstances?

- What inheritance do you envision giving to your children? All of your estate, a specific amount, or nothing at all?

CHAPTER SEVEN

Values Alignment

Now that we've addressed many of the practical, tactical, and relational issues faced by wealth creators, it's time to explore some of the deeper psychological and even spiritual implications of wealth. As we've seen, wealth creators face unique challenges when it comes to managing their financial lives and their relationships, but they also have unique opportunities to *maximize* their lives.

In the next three chapters, I'll ask you to set aside some time to go deep and examine thoughts and feelings that we don't often make time for—perhaps because we're afraid of the changes we might have to make if we acknowledge a disconnect between what we truly believe and the life we're living. Put aside your hesitations, and trust that if you do the thinking and feeling work in Chapters Seven, Eight, and Nine, you'll come out on the other side with a game plan for a truly happy, connected, fulfilled, and wealthy life.

What Do You Value Most?

The first step to achieving a life of meaning and purpose as a wealth creator is discovering what your core values are. I define "core values" as your unique operating system, kind of like the DNA in every cell of your body that regulates how your body functions. Core values are hard-wired—they define, in a very real sense, who you are and where you thrive. Many of our natural tendencies and talents spring from our core values.

Through a discovery process, which we'll go over in detail in this chapter, I've come to understand my own core values, which include courage, faith, presence, wholeness, innovation, and generosity. My values tend to fall within the broader motivations of love and wisdom. It is my innate desire to be a voice of loving wisdom in whatever circumstance I find myself. I also value knowledge and have advanced certifications in a field that is data-driven, but it takes more effort for me to work on knowledge projects than it does to build relationships, which feels almost effortless for me.

It's common for your values to become clearer over time as your life unfolds and your capacity to understand yourself grows. The pace of self-discovery and "knowing" is different for everyone, but as Aristotle once said, "Knowing yourself is the beginning of all wisdom." In my own values journey, I've come to appreciate how my understanding of what makes me tick has been illuminated and become more nuanced. I'm able to better articulate my values at this stage of my life then when I was younger. Some of that comes with the perspective of time and life experiences.

You may wonder if your core values at age 25 are different than what you value at 40, 50, or after retirement. Life circumstances may shift our understanding or the expression of our core values for a time, which may lead us to believe that they have changed, but actually, we may simply have healed certain wounds or uncovered a truth about ourselves that brings our core values back into focus.

Core values are critically important, sometimes hard to grasp, and a gray area for many people. I've found that through the process of discovering our values, we can recognize deep truths about ourselves and begin to understand how our money and our values align. How am I wired to respond almost effortlessly in certain circumstances, and where do I have to exert more effort to fulfill a value that is important to me? Where might I need to prioritize one value over another, depending on a specific situation or time in my life? How can I shift my spending and investing decisions so they are in harmony with what I value most?

As you recognize what you value most, your definition of success may change: Understanding what the money is for in your life may reveal paths you haven't considered or shift your mindset to focus on different values, such as freedom, community, fun, or creativity, as new measuring sticks for success. For those interested in philanthropy and generosity, discovering your core values is the key to putting your money where your heart is. If you want to avoid the debilitating downsides of wealth, you need to discover the purpose of *your* wealth. Your values are a compass guiding you to a life of meaning, so wealth can produce the best outcomes for you, your relationships, and the world around you.

(Many thanks to Lynn Taylor, founder of Taylor Protocols, for his work on the subject of core values, which has influenced my ideas and helped me on my journey of understanding.)

Values Discovery

In order to understand our core values and answer the question "What's the money for?," we begin by exploring fundamental truths about ourselves:

- Who are you? Who do you love? What is your life about?
- What stage in life are you at right now? What are the challenges and opportunities of this time and place?
- What are the really big things you want to experience, do, see, or create in your life?

Take some time to think about these questions and write down your thoughts. The answers to these questions can help us hone in on the values we hold most dear. One of my favorite questions to ask wealth creators as we begin our work together is this: "Money is a means to an end, a means to achieving something important to you. What is most important to you?"

There are several areas worth considering as you begin sleuthing for evidence and clues as to where your values reside: those closest to you, your fondest hopes and greatest fears, and the make-believe world of no financial constraints. If you take away money as a constraint in your life and assume that you had all you needed to be successful, what would you do differently personally, professionally, financially? These potential future outcomes are additional nuggets of insight to explore for gold. If you achieve that desired result, what will it do for your life? What benefit will it bring? Why is it so important? Typically, the answers to these questions are the buds of core values starting to bloom.

Asking and answering these fundamental questions about ourselves, our lives, and our dreams are the beginning of what I call an "Ideal Outcomes" conversation. My goal is to help every wealth creator recognize the values they want to build their life on and to have a vision for their own personal "Ideal Outcome"—when you look back on your life, will you experience a sense of satisfaction that your choices have reflected your most treasured values and your ideal experience? Money plays a huge part in our most important decisions—how we spend our time, who we spend it with, the experiences we can have, and our sense of purpose in the world. Money and values go hand in hand.

An important mind shift occurs through this personal discovery process: Money itself (earning it, growing it, controlling it) is no longer the objective. Instead, money becomes energy and a tool to achieve the outcomes you care most about. These outcomes can be tangible things like education, travel, and family experiences, as well as bigger concepts such as freedom, community, generosity, and joy.

Wealth does increase choices and time freedom to do and experience the things you really love. While almost everyone thinks about what they care about most from time to time, many highly successful couples and individuals don't carve out the time to think really deeply about these questions and prioritize what matters most to them. Begin by setting aside at least 30 minutes to engage with the Values Discovery Questionnaire in this chapter. Some categories may require more thought than others: Perhaps you instantly respond to Achievement, Family, or Service as a value that's a high priority in your life. Other values such as Abundance, Emotional Health, or Spirituality may require more time for introspection.

Take all the time you need to think about the values—what they mean, how they show up in your actions and decisions, and how certain values you hold dear may or may not be a priority in your life right now. In the column labeled "Importance," rate each value's importance to you on a 1–5 scale (1 being the lowest importance, 5 the highest). In the "Evidence" column, rate each value on how it is currently showing up in your life right now. Keep in mind that the "Importance" rating can be aspirational— perhaps Communication, Adventure, or Fun are of great importance to you, but they aren't finding a prominent place in your life right now because of time constraints. They can still receive a high "Importance" rating while having a lower rating in the "Evidence" column. If there are values that you hold dear that do not appear on the questionnaire, I would encourage you to add those values (and rate them) in the blank spaces provided. Once you have rated all the values, find those with a 5 rating in the "Importance" column. Circle or make a list of your top five most important values based on this process, then rank these values in order of importance.

Pause here and take all the time you need to complete the Values Discovery Questionnaire. Remember, there are no wrong answers—only the answers that are true for your life and beliefs.

Walking Your Talk

Now that you've completed the important work of rating your values, the Values Discovery Questionnaire results will be your guide through Chapters Seven, Eight, and Nine of this book. Understanding which values are truly your top priority will help you make important decisions about who you care about and who you want to take care of, who you are now, and who you wish to become in the future. Disparities between the

Table 7.1   Values Discovery Questionnaire

VALUE	IMPORTANCE (SCALE 1–5)	EVIDENCE (SCALE 1–5)
Abundance		
Accuracy		
Achievement		
Adventure		
Altruism		
Authenticity		
Beauty		
Clarity		
Commitment		
Communication		
Community		
Compassion		
Courage		
Creativity		
Education		
Emotional Health		
Empathy		
Family		
Flexibility		
Freedom		
Friendship		
Frugality		
Fulfillment		
Fun		
Generosity		
Health		
Holistic Living		
Honesty		
Humor		

(continued)

Table 7.1   Values Discovery Questionnaire (*continued*)

VALUE	IMPORTANCE (SCALE 1–5)	EVIDENCE (SCALE 1–5)
Integrity		
Intimacy		
Joy		
Leadership		
Legacy		
Love		
Loyalty		
Nature		
Openness		
Partnership		
Perseverance		
Personal Growth		
Physical Appearance		
Power		
Privacy		
Professionalism		
Recognition		
Respect		
Romance		
Security		
Self-Care		
Service		
Spirituality		
Trust		
Wisdom		

"Importance" and "Evidence" ratings for certain key values can help you understand where you aren't "walking your talk"—in other words, your values aren't guiding your decisions as they could (and perhaps should) be.

Hold on to your Values Discovery Questionnaire, and start noticing where these values show up and influence your daily life and where your values and your choices are incongruent. Consider writing or printing out a list of your most important values and keeping it someplace you will see it—perhaps on the refrigerator or your computer—as a daily reminder.

Let's examine how an awareness of your most deeply held values can and should influence your financial decisions. Through my coach training, I've come to understand how my thoughts lead to emotional responses, and those emotions lead to actions or behaviors. Your money EQ, or emotional intelligence around money, is very much a function of your thoughts.

My thoughts and your thoughts are shaped tremendously by the values that are core to who we are. When I recognize how my thoughts about money connect to my innate values wiring, then my emotional responses to money can become healthier, which leads to improved downstream decision-making.

Without a values-defined lodestar guiding your thoughts, you may find yourself stuck in the patterns of "Control," "Concern," or "Cautious" behavior responses discussed in Chapter Four that are counterproductive to achieving your fondest hopes and dreams for your life. Your values are the sweet center that brings purpose and meaning to the spending, saving, and sharing roles that money plays in your life.

In my own life, I value being generous with my money, and I strive to be open-minded and open-hearted, proactively looking for opportunities to act out of a sense of compassion and love. At times, I too can get emotionally swamped by fear and anxiety about the balance in my brokerage account, which leads me to be more cautious. Instead of acting, I will justify my need for additional financial security, telling myself that another opportunity to give will show up later. When I don't follow clear and direct signals coming from my deeply held value of generosity, I realize I am not achieving my ideal outcome.

Practically speaking, how will the core values you have identified play out in financial decisions regarding your household—do you have a spouse or partner, children, or other relations who you wish to support financially? What about obligations and aspirations around education, family experiences, and travel? Do you plan to offer financial support for your grown children, your parents, your siblings, or others? Money is not an end, but a means to achieving something of importance. What is most important to you?

A couple I worked with who were real estate investors strongly valued education, as many wealth creators do. There was a great disparity between their financial resources and those of their extended family. Most of their siblings had struggled financially, and the couple experienced a lot of guilt around how unfair it was that their parents and others in the family didn't enjoy the lifestyle benefits they had achieved through wealth.

Unfortunately, when they gave generous checks to parents and siblings, they found that the amount never seemed to be enough or the money didn't serve the purposes they had had in mind. For example, they hoped that the money could be used to cover outstanding credit card balances, but they found within a short period of time that overspending had returned, and sometimes had become even worse, with the result that family members expected even more financial support from them in the future.

This couple wanted the money they gave to their extended family to align better with outcomes they cared about. Feelings of frustration had built up on both sides over the years, and they were looking for a different way to provide help. That's where focusing on their value of education came into play. By offering to pay the college expenses of their nieces and nephews, they were able to honor their value of education and give the next generation of their family a pathway to greater opportunities in life. They felt good about investing in the long-term success of the family at large in this way. When spending decisions are connected to a value, you honor who you are and what you care about.

Travel is another opportunity to incorporate important values like generosity and family. A long-term client of mine in Seattle wanted to be generous and create deeper bonds of connection with her extended family. They mostly lived on the East Coast, and she didn't get to see them very often. She was also a big fan of the Seattle Seahawks football team, so she decided to fly all of her extended family members to Florida to watch the Seahawks play. Most of her other family members had very different financial means and could not have had that experience otherwise. She generously covered all their travel, hotel, and meal expenses, and she created an important bonding experience and a treasured memory for the whole family by letting her values guide her spending decisions.

Observe your expectations, feelings, and desires regarding your closest family and friend relationships. How do you want your money to influence those relationships? Consider how values such as Service, Adventure, Fun, Education, and Intimacy might influence your choices around family learning experiences, paying for college, travel, vacation properties, and social outings. Making financial choices aligned with your deepest values will help you realize your Ideal Outcome for these relationships.

As we discussed in Chapter Five, it is especially important for couples to spend time discussing and comparing their most dearly held values. Some partners may discover that they have differing core values, putting them at odds when it comes to financial decision-making. Remember James and Mary, who found that their differing value positions—one focused on frugality, the other on family experiences—became a point of great contention within their marriage.

Couples need to set aside time to discuss what is most important to each partner, not just forge ahead with an independently created vision that you hope your partner agrees with. After having many of these conversations over the years, I can't tell you the number of times that a couple will say how important it was to hear each other talk about their money objectives and give each other the gift of a shared vision for their ideal future together. While financial security is normally on the list, it is rarely the reason why they are working hard, building wealth, or getting up each day. Aligning your values with your spouse/partner's values is a critical step toward Living Fully and achieving a mutual ideal outcome for your life together.

Kelle and I went through a process similar to this, examining our unique individual values and then discussing the shared values for our relationship as a married couple. Our shared values include Authenticity, Commitment, and Legacy. To memorialize it, we even painted a picture together that is mounted on the wall in our bedroom, regularly reminding us of our united values.

Fear Factor

The next step in aligning your values with your money is taking a good hard look at both your fondest hopes and dreams and where your biggest fears reside, personally, professionally, and financially. Creating your own definition of success can lead you to a better understanding of your hopes and dreams, and to values such as Generosity, Legacy, and Courage. Likewise, worries and concerns about the personal, professional, and financial parts of life can guide us to identify important values that we may be neglecting.

Wealth creators can become so focused on the all-consuming act of making, investing, and protecting the money that hitting their number becomes the only measure of success. As we discussed in Chapter One, maximizing your return on life hinges on a broader definition of success, including things like staying healthy, enjoying close relationships with family and friends, treasuring experiences rather than stuff, finding joy in generosity and learning opportunities, and understanding what the money is for in your life. The top five values you have identified in the Values Assessment Questionnaire can unlock a new definition of what "success" means for you and help you spend, give, and invest your money purposefully.

A few years ago, I had the chance to meet Dave Cotter, founder and, at the time, chief executive officer (CEO) of a start-up called SquareHub, a social networking platform for families. In Dave, I saw a real-life example of embracing values to create a new definition of success: living life fully and with authenticity, making meaningful connections, being generous, and allowing yourself to be vulnerable to life's possibilities.

But Dave arrived at his values-driven lifestyle the hard way: At age 41, he had a stroke that nearly killed him. Dave had been grinding away at a high-level position at Amazon, followed by creating and selling a start-up company. He had neglected his relationships, which led to the end of his 10-year marriage, and neglected his health. He was disconnected from his three daughters. He was making plenty of money, but he was not happy. In fact, he said he felt empty, alone, and unfulfilled.

Dave didn't let a good crisis go to waste. Following his near-death experience, he reexamined his priorities. "I have an interesting sense of joy and ease that is foreign to my prior way of life," he told me. "Five years ago I would have been extremely stressed out and needing sedation. Instead, I'm happy, having fun, and feel fulfilled." Today, he spends more time with his daughters, makes them lunch every day, and takes them to school. Taking care of important personal relationships is where your life should begin, he realized. His failure to do so cost him his marriage and compromised his performance at work.

"My mistake was, I set a trajectory and expectation for my life early on and then went into grind mode," Dave told me. "Money can insulate you, but it also creates different problems." One of the most significant changes in his thinking after the stroke was shifting his mentality from "get" to "give." By shifting his attention to helping others, he stays focused on relationships instead of stuff. He recovered from his near-fatal stroke with one clear, simple desire in mind: "I want to be remembered for raising three amazing daughters, and for helping people," he said.

Dave has clearly embraced his values of Family, Generosity and Service, and allowed these values to guide his career, life, and financial choices going forward after his stroke. Sometimes it takes a frightening experience to change our mindset. Luckily, we don't have to face death personally in order to identify areas of our lives where things aren't working optimally. Our fears and worries can give us clues to values we may be neglecting. What do you worry about, both personally and professionally? What is your greatest fear? The thoughts that keep us up at night are key to understanding what we value most and where wealth can do the most good in our lives.

I've found that risk is an important element in embracing our deeply held values. Many times, the things that we enjoy the most and that bring us the most meaning aren't sure things and come with some form of uncertainty and risk. When you consider undertaking something new, sweaty palms and a healthy fear of failure can signal that you're on the right track. The very existence of this book can be attributed to dreaming bigger than I thought possible and putting myself in a risky position with an unsure outcome. I believe that's often where meaning and purpose reside.

Putting Your Money Where Your Heart Is

Discovering core values often leads wealth creators to a newfound sense of purpose when it comes to generosity and philanthropy. In other words: putting your money where your heart is.

One of my core values is Compassion, and about five years ago, I realized I didn't have a clue how to discover needs or causes in the world that I could care about. I knew people who were driven to raise money to fight cancer because they had a loved one who had battled it, or who had some other personal connection to a charitable organization. I wasn't naturally drawn to any particular cause, and that bothered me. It sounds crazy, but there was a point where I started digging into my own past to check whether I had any emotional connection to a disease that could create a passionate connection.

A friend of mine referred me to Heather, a philanthropic advisor, for help. I told her that giving just felt like a check-writing exercise, and that I wanted to connect emotion to generosity. She suggested taking my wife and me on what she called a "heart tour." I wasn't familiar with the concept, and the words "heart tour" piqued my interest. Heather explained that she would take us to various nonprofits to visit, meet the staff, and see what needs they were filling.

On that tour, we visited the Union Gospel Mission addiction and recovery program in Seattle. We attended the graduation of a group of women from the program. Needless to say, we were incredibly moved by these women, both their vulnerability and their courage to face life's steepest challenges and choose to keep fighting. Kelle and I were hooked.

Shortly after this, my wife started teaching addiction recovery classes at the women's shelter. Late in the evening, we would go out on their search-and-rescue van to provide food, blankets, and basic necessities to the most vulnerable residents of our city, the homeless population. We saw first-hand, under city bridges and in parks, what homelessness looked like and smelled like, and it wrecked us for the better.

Heather later took us to Africa as part of a discovery-and-research process in her role as the executive director for a local foundation. We had one of the most moving experiences of our lives when we met Michael in the bush of Uganda, living in a small hut with no food. Michael was one of the many child-headed households that exist across Africa, due to the ravages of war and disease. He was only about 15 years old and was responsible for his three younger sisters.

Along with our friends, Eric and Heather, we contributed to the education, safety, and care of this young man (and his sisters), who had no education and no real skills. We came home with changed hearts, and when that happens, money flows intuitively. Generosity didn't feel forced, emotionless, or something I had to be convinced of. It was, as my friend Paul Shoemaker calls it, a "Can't Not Do."

When you uncover the values-based motivators in your life, money moves effortlessly in that direction and decision-making is simplified. Through intentional introspection and discovery, you will begin to understand where your deeply held values are already guiding your actions, and which values are still aspirational.

Your most important values are a beacon that can light up the pathway to your most important objectives in life. Without these guiding principles, you can grope in the dark, not knowing what purpose wealth has in your life, or how to make meaning of money.

Remember to regularly review your list of the top five most important values: They will guide your choices and help you discover where you can have a significant impact through generosity. Values anchor us on our path to Living Fully.

CONSIDER THESE QUESTIONS ABOUT YOUR CORE VALUES:

- Which values are nonnegotiable in your life, and why?
- What value is currently aspirational, which you would like to emphasize more in the future?
- Do you have shared values with your spouse or partner? Are they written down? What type of support or facilitation for that conversation might you need?
- Have you experienced a generosity moment or event in your life that was guided by your values?

CHAPTER EIGHT

Your Highest Calling

The gift of wealth opens an amazing world of possibility. The initial discovery work we have explored in this book around success, money EQ, and relationships examines the question, "What is the money for?" Understanding your values shifts the focus to "What is my life for?"

If the pursuit of money has been your measuring stick for success, how do you evaluate your life once wealth has been achieved? How do you find meaning and purpose? A "calling" is a gravitational pull that draws you forward into a life of service to something bigger than yourself. This chapter will help you discover your unique contribution to the world, really let yourself dream bigger than you thought possible, and realize the impact that only you can make.

The pathway to a higher calling and purpose hasn't been a straight line in my life. It has unfolded like a present unwrapped over many years. Only through the lens of hindsight can I clearly see the arc of my story, through its many twists and turns. The concept of the hero's journey mirrors what I've experienced in the process of understanding my calling.

In the hero's journey, there is a call to adventure caused by a disruption in life that forces you out of your equilibrium state. You embark into the unknown, where mentors and helpers emerge to help you through the trials and challenges that come. Ultimately, there is a revelation that causes a death and rebirth experience, and reconstruction and transformation begin, culminating in a return to the known world and a new role in life. I've found that just like an archetypal hero, as I have taken on new adventures and become the lead actor in my own story, my higher purpose has been revealed.

This was certainly true 10 years into building and running my company, Highland Private Wealth Management. Highland's purpose in my life has always been much more than just a job: It has been a painter's canvas used by God to mold, heal, and transform me.

Just past the first decade of Highland's profitable existence, I hit a wall emotionally, mentally, and physically. The accumulated years of long hours, volatile financial markets, managing employees, and serving newly wealthy clients were exhilarating as the business thrived—and simultaneously, sucking me dry. As the chief cook and bottle washer, I pretty much performed every task imaginable at one time or another, relying on raw grit, persistence, and the fear of failure to single-handedly will the company forward.

A key impetus for my intense drive came from my former bosses, who had told me during that ominous yearly review back in 1999 that I didn't have what it took to ever run my own business, let alone succeed in the financial services industry. Immature as it was, I made a vow to prove them wrong, to dodge the high probability of failure faced by most start-up businesses. I was going to survive at all costs.

And costly it was. When you live from a place of anxiety, fear, worry, and a "me against the world" mental and emotional state, you spend a huge amount of energy. It's like being on a treadmill, your legs running as fast as they can but never gaining any ground. This catabolic form of energy gave me the momentum to accomplish a great deal in the short run, making me feel successful, but at a long-term cost to my health and wellness.

The years started blurring together, and the personal impact of achieving this mission based on "survival" began taking a bigger and bigger toll on my life. I was quickly running out of gas, and I desperately needed a new North Star to guide the journey ahead: a new destination, a clearer purpose, a better "why." In other words, I needed a higher calling that would draw my life forward into a happier, more fulfilling future.

I started doing some personal healing and self-improvement work. I had been living in black and white, and I wanted to experience living in Technicolor. Highland represented a huge part of my identity at that time, but what I was looking for transcended a business mission or vision. I began to look inward instead of outward. This was a time of self-discovery, of healing from the emotional and psychological wounds of my past, and of embracing my faith in a power greater than myself.

My spiritual journey led to ask three important questions that I believe are the key to finding your higher calling: Who are you? Why do you exist? What is your unique contribution?

Who Are You?

I really didn't know the answer to this question. My life was busy, and I spent a great deal of time performing, achieving, and living externally.

By that, I mean that I lived for external rewards and the approval of others, as a validation of who I was and my worth. Until I started pulling back the layers of my life and examining my intentions, I hadn't realized that many of my behaviors, such as perfectionism and control, were coping skills I'd honed to help me achieve externally motivated "success."

Starting to discover my "who" put me in direct contact with my failures, worries, and fears, which were painful to face. This process of discovery also helped me to recognize my personal achievements, gifts, talents, and core values; the essence of who I was at a soul level of being; my authentic self.

There is a saying that goes, "The fear of staying the same has to be greater than the fear of change before any movement will occur." It took time and various counselors, coaches, and life-planning experts to guide and help me through this process. It often felt daunting, and I wanted and needed someone to show me how to do it. My wife had experienced her own journey of discovery and was a huge support and encouragement in leading the way. Digging down to the heart and soul level can be tough.

I had spent years distracting myself with work and personal achievement because it was just easier. However, once the lid came off and I ventured into the unknown, I found an infusion of positive energy moving me forward. It became a personal mission to understand myself and grow. I read everything I could about core values and learning to both understand and love myself for who I was—not who I wished I was, but who I was in the present moment. Being "enough" was an interesting concept for me because it went against the other tensions of approval and the world's definition of success, including financial success.

Until we ask and answer the question "Who am I?" we can't align our money to a life of meaning and purpose. The path of least resistance for many people is hiding their authentic self, keeping secrets, and living life in isolation. Wealth and success contribute mightily to this end.

I facilitate a men's group at our church called Genesis Process. At the heart of the program is the idea of being known, by yourself and others, in a loving and supportive community. For men in particular, looking under the proverbial hood to see who we really are is a scary concept. It's very powerful when we realize we aren't alone in our fears and worries, we aren't the only ones who have failed and have regrets, and that we really do have dreams and hopes, even if some of those dreams have been nearly suffocated by life circumstances over time.

Years ago, I was uncomfortable, uncertain, and embarrassed to talk about myself and who I was at my core. While I'm not fluent yet, I've gained a sense of ease in accepting and appreciating the person I am. The attributes and characteristics of John include loving, innovative, competitive, courageous, adventuresome, spiritual, athletic, generous, intelligent, curious, fun, inspirational, healthy, brave, loyal, and sensitive.

Part of my "who" also entails the challenge areas that I'm working to improve, such as perfectionist, controlling, insecure, and anxious. There are also many roles I fill in life that create the external expression of John, including son, father, grandfather, husband, friend, entrepreneur, coach, writer, facilitator, and child of God.

Keep in mind that purposeful self-examination takes reflection time and journaling. You may also consider discussing your ideas with a trusted confidant, who can provide perspective. The following are questions that will aid in your process of self-discovery:

- What are the top five talents, skills, and competencies that you are most proud of?
- What are the top five personal values that you would never sacrifice?
- What are the core beliefs you have about yourself? (These may include beliefs that you would be embarrassed to admit to or speak out loud.)
- If a close friend or spouse had to write your obituary today, what would it say about you? What would you want it to say?

Why Do You Exist?

For me, this is a spiritual question about my personal faith and dependence on God for everything. Your answer may be different, including just enjoying life. Were you a cosmic accident or part of a divine plan? Coming to grips with your reason for existence sets a course for the journey ahead.

"Why do I exist?" is a tough question for many people and something we don't think much about. Even if you were raised within a religious tradition, the diverse concepts, definitions, and opinions on the subject can leave you confused and just plain stuck when it comes to finding real answers to why you are here on planet Earth. This kind of introspection requires wrestling with your thoughts on life, God or a higher power, and ultimately spirituality.

We commonly talk about the resilience and power of the "human spirit." Many believe that we have soul and spirit in us. For me, soul represents the essence of who we are, and spirit represents our connection to a source greater than ourselves. The language of that spirit or spirituality is love, grace, forgiveness, and joy.

The Danish philosopher Søren Kierkegaard wrote that people first attempt to attain fulfillment by acquiring stuff, all of which ultimately becomes meaningless. Seeking deeper fulfillment, people turn to deeds or causes, perhaps by helping others or by following their conscience. That too will ultimately prove meaningless, Kierkegaard says, without faith, a fixed belief in something beyond the material world—in other words, a higher power.

I also believe there is a higher power, a higher source that connects all things and provides the framework that makes sense of this life. I don't believe that I am an accident, or that my life is coincidental, and I don't believe that is true for you either.

It only takes viewing the majestic mountains outside of my living room window or feeling the simple rhythm of my breathing and heartbeat to be deeply grateful for my life and believe that there is a God. Perhaps your beliefs about a higher power are different than mine, but I think that every human can sense a connection with something bigger than themselves, whether it's through nature or art or our collective humanity.

We weren't created just to exist, but to *Live Fully*. Just existing sounds horrible, and yet many people find themselves in that rut. Why? Because stagnation or the status quo is safer somehow. It's what we know, and it comes with an outcome we understand and feel in control of. Yes, Living Fully is inherently risky. We all try valiantly to eliminate risk in our lives, in our portfolios, but we inherently know that more risk provides greater returns, both for our portfolios and in our lives.

I want to encourage you to create a bigger definition of why you were created and exist. If your "why" is to grab all the money you can while you're here on Earth, I believe that you will be disappointed in the ultimate outcome and the legacy you will leave when you are gone.

However, if you embrace risk, which requires faith in something bigger than yourself, opportunities open up that are limited only by your imagination. That's why this question is so central to finding our highest calling.

The answer I found to be true for me is that my purpose here is to be of service to someone or something greater than myself. I want my authentic self to be expressed and given in service as long as I'm physically capable of doing so.

HERE ARE A FEW QUESTIONS TO PONDER AND WRITE ABOUT THAT MAY HELP YOU UNDERSTAND WHY YOU ARE HERE:

- How would you describe the purpose of your life?
- What is your definition of spirituality?
- What are the deep yearnings of your heart?
- When do you feel most alive?

What Is Your Unique Contribution?

The final question that will lead you to your highest calling asks you to discover the one-of-a-kind contribution that only you can make. Pinpointing your unique contribution to the world involves introspection, examining what brings you joy and fulfillment, and understanding what makes your whole being light up with energy.

I liken this process to finding the sweet spot on a wooden baseball bat. For nonbaseball players, the sweet spot is a location on the barrel of the bat where the ball will fly the farthest when struck. You can find that spot in several ways, including using a solid stick or rod to strike the bat at different locations up and down along it. The sweet spot will produce a different vibration and sound when you strike it. You can also test for it by hitting ball after ball off the suspected sweet spots, noting the distance and location differences.

This discovery process requires the use of all your senses. Similarly, unearthing your unique contribution will require a deep dive into your thoughts, memories, emotions, and intuition. It may also require courage to accept the unexpected answers you find there.

In my journey to find my highest calling, I began to recognize that the experience of starting Highland had been just what I had hoped for: a spiritual journey of discovery, where I could know and understand myself better and feel a deeper sense of fulfillment in life. I realized as I worked out my new "why"—both personally and for my company's existence—that my desire had always been to help people beyond just managing their money.

Building financial plans and making sure that my clients stayed rich was never enough for me. I always felt that Highland was a relationship firm that happened to be in the wealth management industry. As I engaged in conversations to understand my clients' values and support their objectives, advising them on intimate and critical parts of their lives, they would often share very personal details about marriage and relationship challenges, identity struggles, and other emotional aspects connected to money.

I found myself in the position of a confidant, sharing my own experiences and stories to help my clients work through their pain points. And not all of these conversations were about pain—many were about hopes and dreams. I loved to hear what clients really wanted for their lives, and I enjoyed strategizing how to help them get there, to experience life in a fuller way.

I realized I was experiencing an evolution of my "why"—I was filling two roles. I was doing the job that I trained for as a financial consultant, offering advice and expertise on money matters. But I was also helping my clients process other deep and important issues, and in many cases, that was the most valuable and unique service I could provide. I recognized that my clients needed a coach to help them find the answers they were looking for within themselves.

I decided to embark on professional coach training. The yearlong training program gave me a process to work with, tools and techniques to become a better listener, methods to ask more empowering questions, and the confidence to understand when I had my consulting hat on in a discussion and when I had on my coaching hat.

About halfway through the training, we had to pick a subspecialty for additional training. When I signed up for the training course, I thought for sure that my ultimate role would be in executive coaching. Executive coaching was the safe answer for me, something that would be easy to explain when people asked me why I was pursuing this training.

During a weekend on-site training experience, I had a dream that confirmed something I'd been feeling in my gut but was unwilling to say out loud: I was going to be a spiritual coach. Spiritual coaching wasn't about religion. It was about helping others do the inner work necessary to find true meaning in life, to discover what God uniquely gifted each of us to do, and then to break away from the impediments to doing it.

I was nervous even talking about the idea with my classmates because I was a business guy, and I felt pressure to stay where I belonged: in the business lane, keeping up the image I'd created for myself over the years. Offering my clients the services of an executive coach, in addition to my wealth management expertise, would create curiosity, but no difficult questions. On the other hand, telling someone I was a spiritual coach was decidedly uncomfortable territory.

But the truth was that I had been having what I referred to as "meaningful conversations" for many years with my clients. I had a special ability to really see what was going on inside of people's lives. Sometimes I could hear the pangs of their souls expressed as frustration, anger, or helplessness. I could see their potential to experience a better return on life, and I wanted to help free them from the obstacles that blocked them if I could.

I also realized that I had special skills in facilitating difficult conversations between couples, and relationship coaching was another area where I excelled. When our coach training program asked for volunteers to role-play a relationship-coaching scenario in front of the class, I did it effortlessly.

It's interesting that we often find our calling in areas where we have practical experience and passion, and I'd been helping couples work through money and life issues for years. I also noticed that exercising this ability generated a great deal of energy for me. This is another clue to recognizing your unique contribution. Helping people get unstuck and seeing them move toward a bigger definition for their life, in a healthy way, created a feeling like electricity within me. I could feel it exploding in my body.

Callings come with clues: energy, experiences, an emerging skill, talent, or passion, or even something that feels risky can tell us that we're on the right track.

All of my professional experience up to this point had been in working with wealth creators, managing money, guiding and stewarding the financial lives of very successful people. It was risky for me to step into this new area. What would people say? Why not just stay focused on wealth management? What if it doesn't work, I look stupid, or no one cares?

Risk in our Life Portfolio is consistent with risk in our investment portfolio. The more risk you take, the better the returns. I've found over the years that most people want stock market returns at bond market volatility. In other words, they want all the upside and little to no downside in their portfolio. However, even novice investors know that risk and return go hand in hand. That's also true in life. Experiencing a higher return on life usually comes with risking something: reputation, time, and even money.

After the insights I gained about my skills in relationship coaching and the path leading me toward being a spiritual coach, I finally was able to give voice to my new "why" and fully realize my unique contribution. At a leadership retreat in 2016, the facilitator asked us to write down our goals for the coming year, why we wanted to accomplish them, what we expected to get out of achieving them, and what was keeping us from doing it.

When asked to share what I'd written, I blurted out: "I'm going to start offering coaching services to individuals and couples around money and life purpose issues." Immediately, several hands shot up, and four guys announced, "I need that!" Once you live into what you were created for, doors and opportunities open up. Words become intentions that become reality. I've since been able to work with many high-achieving couples and individuals in a wealth-counseling setting, and that experience feeds me in new ways. Writing this book has been another part of realizing and living my highest calling.

Often, we make excuses not to live fully, and fear can keep us from accepting our highest calling once we recognize the contribution that we are uniquely suited to make. This was the case for me for a long time. I wanted to stay in the safety zone, thinking about my potential but not stepping into the vision fully, and staying an observer. The addition of wealth creates both opportunities and challenges in seeking our highest calling.

Wealth is not a cure-all: If you lacked passion at your job before the money arrived, it will not cure that ailment. A middle-aged executive I was coaching was not happy at his job before the money arrived from a family business sale. The windfall allowed him to quit his job, but that created a new pressure to find something to be passionate about in his life. At first, he thought, "Hey, I can now leave the job I don't like, and that is great!" But now he wonders, "Will I ever find something that fulfills me that I can really sink my teeth into and contribute to?" Money hasn't fixed the underlying issue: a lack of purpose and identity.

Time freedom and having choices can be positive, but wealth creators may find themselves with so many opportunities that they feel overwhelmed and unable to choose. It can feel like anything is possible, which is a wonderful gift, but choosing can be very difficult for some.

I remember an experience with one of my early coaching clients, who was struggling to find identity in his life, almost feeling numb about the various alternatives in front of him. Choices were plentiful, but there wasn't a mechanism for him to decide what the right choice was. I asked him, "When was the last time you did something that felt risky? When did you do something that had a cost to it if it didn't work out, and consequences?"

We can try to take away all of the risk and volatility, to feel more in control and safe, but we also take away all of the upside, the returns, the big rewards. I've found that risk is an important element in finding meaning and purpose. Many times, the things that we enjoy the most and bring us the most meaning aren't sure bets; they come with some form of uncertainty and risk. Sweaty palms and the fear of failure may signal that we are near the place we belong.

WORK THROUGH THE FOLLOWING QUESTIONS, THROUGH PONDERING AND WRITING, TO DISCOVER YOUR UNIQUE CONTRIBUTION:

- What are your innate interests and gifts that you could describe as passions?
- Describe your best day: What are you doing, seeing, feeling, experiencing, contributing? What are the things that bring up tremendous positive energy even when thinking about them?
- What roles have you had in life? Which ones have felt "right," closest to your true self, or even a "calling"?
- How would you describe your fondest hope for the future? Does this vision for your future scare you at all? If not, is the vision big enough or exciting enough?

Maximizing Your Return on Life

A few years ago, I met with a prospective client, and after hearing about the unique relationship building process we have at Highland and our mission to free people to live fully, Steve asked me, "John, are you living fully?" This was a moment of confirmation in my life as I realized, "Yes, I am living fully!"

I had embraced risk, started a company, embraced risk again, and discovered my unique contribution. I was healing from past wounds and living in the moment. I could say a resounding "yes" to that question, and it felt really good. It also made me realize that my job was not only to talk about living life fully, but to model it.

We all want a life where our energy is high and the days fly by because we are completely engaged in a fulfilling contribution to our relationships and the world. The gift of wealth can enable us to realize big dreams and goals, at the confluence of where values, skills, talents, interests, and background meet the magnitude of a mission, leading us to meaningful and purposeful experiences. However, there is a missing element.

The role of faith and spirituality has been the backbone for my courage to navigate the stewardship of my life and career. I was raised in a Christian home, attend church regularly, and believe in God. Belief in something greater than yourself can be justified and explained only as we experience outcomes that are beyond our own abilities. Much of my story can be explained only through faith. The circumstances that led to forming Highland, the clients we serve, and my personal transformation are only a few examples of this.

The Jewish faith has a concept called "shalom," a word that loosely translates as "peace"—a state when all things, relationships, and God are in alignment, the way they were intended to be. To flourish is another biblical concept, which means to live into who God uniquely created you to be. Both of these ideas simplify and clarify the "why" behind my life and give me the confidence to continually seek God's will for my life, knowing I was created with a purpose for my life and the ability to contribute to God's plan for the world.

The latest iteration of what I think of as my "God-calling" is to help wealth creators and those who aspire to create wealth to invest their lives, including their financial resources, in purposeful outcomes. This includes using their gift of wealth in proportion to the blessings received.

I'm attempting to model that with my own life because I've been richly blessed, too. In my case, and because I believe God is the ultimate owner of my wealth, my wife and I have starting tithing on our business—10 percent of Highland's profits now go to charity, as an expression of our shared values of faith and generosity. I'm also using my influence, expertise, and time to teach what I've learned about the thoughtful alignment of money and life from my own personal experience and my career as a wealth counselor.

I believe that we are designed to create and contribute, as long as we are able to do so. You can define this as work that generates wages and compensation or not—vocation and avocation. Whatever "work" drives us fills an important purpose in our lives, which is why I'm not a believer in the concept of retirement.

I don't believe in working until age 45, 55, or 65, and then, with a significant amount of potential to continue contributing to the world, we just put those skills, talents, and experiences on the shelf so we can play golf every day. Maximizing your return on life isn't about playing as many rounds of golf as possible, although I have nothing against playing golf and quite enjoy it. I want my life to matter so much more. I want to contribute everything I can, for as long as I can, leaving nothing in reserve.

When we do the important inner work of discovering who we are, why we exist, and what our unique contribution to the world is, we can realize our highest calling and begin to *live fully*. We increase the odds of winning at the game of money and life when we align the gift of wealth with the best that is in us.

NOW THAT YOU'VE DONE THE DEEP WORK OF UNDERSTANDING WHO YOU ARE, WHY YOU EXIST, AND THE UNIQUE CONTRIBUTION THAT YOU CAN MAKE, GIVE YOURSELF THE FREEDOM TO CONSIDER THE FOLLOWING QUESTIONS:

- Write a list of one to three areas where you feel a "higher calling." What contribution could you make in these areas?
- What is one action (no matter how big or small) you could take that would move you toward that outcome? Remember, this might feel risky, and it may require an investment of time or possibly money.
- Who would be helpful to talk to about your ideas? Who might encourage you and hold you accountable moving forward?

CHAPTER NINE

My Life Portfolio

In my wealth advisory business, Highland Private Wealth Management, the goal is for every client to "Live Fully," integrating wealth and personal life goals. As you redefine success, identify your core values, and begin to recognize your highest calling, you lay the framework to begin Investing Your Life. If we only get one life to live, why not make it a ridiculously amazing one?

Beginning with a practical review of your current financial and life circumstances, you will start to uncover new paths to deeper meaning and purpose in your life, as well as tools to evaluate your progress. Once you understand the various components of your Life Portfolio, including financial, vocational, social, physiological, experiential, intellectual, and spiritual capital, you will understand where to focus needed attention or even make major changes. As your life and your money become aligned, you will come to a personal understanding of what "Living Fully" means to you and answer for yourself the question, "What's the money for?"

About a year ago, we hired a new lead advisor at Highland. He was drawn to the company in part by the concept of thoughtfully aligning money and life. At the time he came on board, I was brimming with excitement about what I was experiencing in my own journey: living fully, coaching wealth creators on wealth and life issues, and witnessing dreams for my life taking shape in living color. After several conversations about my journey of inner healing and discovery, our new hire asked a simple question: Would you consider teaching the Highland team about Living Fully so that we can be more informed and equipped in our own lives? I realized that I'd been so focused on my own journey, I had neglected to share my learning and insights with my own team! Everyone, no matter where they are on the journey of building wealth, can benefit from learning to live fully.

Living Fully

Living Fully is a concept that has intrigued me for many years. I've found that Living Fully can mean very different things to different people. For some people, it has negative connotations, as in, "I have too much on my plate and I'm full and overwhelmed." Or, it can mean "full," like how your whole body feels at the end of a wonderful meal: perfectly content. To some, the concept of Living Fully can seem completely foreign: They have never thoughtfully considered what they want out of life, or they don't believe they can choose to live more deliberately.

Some individuals know they want a different outcome for their life but get stuck in a routine or a job that pays well, but is unfulfilling. Others have limited their ability to live fully by putting constraints on what is possible due to risk aversion, anxiety, lack of alignment with a spouse, or any number of other reasons that keep life on "mute." Many people realize that they are "living the dream," but still don't feel content or fulfilled, while others have a rough outline of aspirational hopes and dreams that don't get much attention or evaluation. Or you might be living someone else's definition of Living Fully, feeling pressure from society or relationships to be and do certain things because you're "supposed to."

Often, wealth creators say that they will live fully once they achieve a certain amount of wealth, but with all their energy focused on work, they never find time to explore the other components of a thoughtfully designed Life Portfolio.

If you have ever felt that "there has to be more," you are not alone. With only one life to live, I'm resolute in being an active participant in my quest to live life to the fullest. I am constantly trying to better understand, experience, and ultimately model Living Fully. In discovering the benefits of living fully for myself, I've found that it's grounded in a holistic and expansive view of wealth that includes your money and all that you are, have, enjoy, and aspire to become. In sum, it's the manifested essence of your life—purpose, legacy, contribution, and connection—that, when aligned thoughtfully, will produce feelings of contentment, hope, joy, peace, and love. These outcomes are, I believe, the sacred objectives of our human experience.

For wealth creators, Living Fully involves integrating your wealth and personal life goals. As discussed in Chapter Seven, knowing and embracing your most important values will guide your journey as you apply wealth to creating a life of meaning and purpose. After you've explored what makes you tick and you begin to understand your unique contribution (Chapter Eight), it's time to build your Life Portfolio.

Most wealth creators understand the concept of a financial portfolio: a group of assets that can include stocks, bonds, mutual funds, commodities, and many other types of investments. The investments in a portfolio are carefully chosen to reflect specific objectives, to mitigate risk, and ultimately to secure positive financial outcomes. I like to apply the idea of a financial portfolio to your life: What assets does your Life Portfolio hold, and how can you leverage those assets to "Live Fully" and maximize the return on your life?

Life Portfolio

One way to look at your life is as an expression of your wealth and abundance. Just as a diversified portfolio includes more than one stock, your wealth is more than just your money. It encompasses various additional inner and outer attributes. "Outer" wealth includes your actual, cold hard cash and financial assets, but also includes vocational, social, and experiential capital. "Inner" wealth includes physiological, intellectual, and spiritual capital. In order to design and live your most extraordinary life, you must first examine and come to value each of these unique assets.

There are seven categories of "capital" that you can invest in your life portfolio:

- Financial Capital (Money)
- Vocational Capital (Work)
- Social Capital (Relationships)
- Experiential Capital (Play)
- Physiological Capital (Health)
- Intellectual Capital (Mind)
- Spiritual Capital (Purpose)

Financial Capital

Financial Capital includes your actual monetary assets and the associated practical, emotional, and physiological benefits of your current financial condition. It's not necessarily about the size of your investment account balances per se, but instead, what the larger financial picture expresses about your life experience. Examples include your level of freedom, peace of mind, confidence, contentment, values alignment, impact, simplicity, and generosity.

In my own life, my wife and I are enjoying increased financial freedom now that our kids are all out of the house, educated, and married. We have passed the peak expenditure zone of raising a family and have entered a new stage of financial prioritizing that is both fun and challenging. I feel much more at peace with how Financial Capital is working in my Life Portfolio than I used to. However, there continues to be a challenging tug of war between lifestyle wants and wishes and my desire to be generous and a good steward of our financial blessings.

Vocational Capital

Vocational Capital represents "work," whether you earn money through your work or not. I like to define work very broadly: as an opportunity for personal achievement that aligns your talent, skills, meaningful contribution, and potential to win; a place where you have a high level of emotional engagement, a mission or a vision in which you passionately believe.

Work has been a growth area for my Life Portfolio in the past several years. I've invested a lot of time and energy on succession planning in my wealth management business and building the framework for a new wealth and life-coaching platform. I know this new chapter in my work is directly tied to a higher calling in my life, and I can't imagine doing anything more meaningful than this. At the same time, while I know deep down that this is the right work for me to be doing at this time, I still have moments of insecurity because of the potential for failure and worry about what other people might think.

Social Capital

Social Capital represents the positive relationships you have with family and friends, the vibrancy of the community where you live, and the reach of your connections and influence. Relationships are a big component of the true "wealth" of life—it's where joy is centered and hope for daily living emanates from.

My wife and I have realized that our Social Capital has suffered some losses over the past few years. Our kids, their friends, and school and sporting events created natural environments for relationships to spark and develop. As our nest has emptied, our community has become smaller than we would like during this period of change. Opportunities to make connections are no longer teed up automatically, and we've realized the importance of making intentional investments in relationships. We are investing more time and effort to connect with friends and family, on a regular basis, to keep our Social Capital at a healthy level.

Experiential Capital

Another word for Experiential Capital is "play." As children, play is as natural as breathing, but adults often let this natural expression of creativity and joy atrophy from disuse. Unlike with Vocational Capital, we aren't embarking on these activities to win, but instead for pure enjoyment or fun. Included in Experiential Capital are travel, adventure, hobbies, and personal interests like learning to play an instrument or painting.

I personally love the "play" stock, and have worked earnestly to increase my Experiential Capital. I've chosen to be a beginner at many different experiences, from coaching baseball with my sons when they were young, to guitar lessons, and most recently, learning to row. It's been five years since I started investing time, effort, and money in rowing, and I've moved steadily up the development curve in both sweep and sculling. It's a magical combination of the beauty of nature and being out on the water, the physical fitness required, the team camaraderie, and the technical nature of the sport that has become a passion. A year ago, I joined a masters team, with many men who have rowed for decades, and I now join them three to four early mornings a week, doing something I truly love.

Physiological Capital

Physiological Capital represents your physical and emotional health and fitness. Keeping our bodies and minds healthy is a critical component of Living Fully, especially as wealth creators are living longer. It's wonderful to have healthy financial resources, but if you don't have the physical or mental health to enjoy your wealth, what's the point? Physiological Capital involves physical fitness—good nutrition, strength, maintaining a healthy weight, and exercise—and emotional health—positive energy, gratitude, happiness, and life satisfaction.

I place a high priority on Physiological Capital, taking care of my body and being mindful of my emotional needs. My physical health is very good, and I feel stronger and in better shape than ever before. I can attribute much of that outcome to high-intensity rowing workouts. I have also been diligent in seeking counseling through extended periods of anxiety as a result of relationship challenges. I've worked hard to build strong and lasting friendships with people who truly know me and understand what I'm trying to accomplish and where I struggle and am fearful. Being known is one of the deep needs we all share, and I've come to realize the importance of that for my emotional health.

Intellectual Capital

Intellectual Capital is your "mind" stock: Our brains produce our every thought, action, memory, feeling, and experience of the world. Investing in your mind includes continuous learning and growth, your level of consciousness, and developing an abundance mindset.

In my life, I've found it's fairly easy to operate on autopilot, where I'm no longer being challenged, learning, or growing in any way. The risk of achieving mastery in any area is that our brains need new challenges; we feel so much better when we learn new things, continue to improve, and avoid becoming complacent.

For example, I've never written a book before. Thought leadership is a completely new environment for me, and I am constantly challenged as I write. I've been on a steep learning curve regarding the publishing business and the development of a team to support my efforts, and even the terminology and expectations are completely new territory. I've been fascinated and learning a ton about the world of agents, deadlines and commitments, public relations platforms, and book cover design. Increasing my investment in Intellectual Capital has helped me embark on a whole new adventure that has already produced huge dividends.

Spiritual Capital

I think of Spiritual Capital as the "purpose" of your life—the investment you have in deeply held beliefs, the connection to a higher power or something greater than yourself, the alignment and expression of your core values, and the legacy you will leave behind. It can be viewed as the bedrock stock of your Life Portfolio because it informs the "why" of your Life Portfolio choices.

I've been drawn to adventures in my life that require courageous faith in a higher power and are grounded in deep and meaningful purpose. I believe that my history and experiences have uniquely prepared me to help wealth creators discover their own paths to a truly wealthy life. For me, this is a calling and a purpose that enrich my Life Portfolio. As the journey of my life unfolds and I continue to grow in my own faith, I can see new opportunities to explore generosity more deeply and find new ways to speak blessing into others' lives.

Building Your Own Life Portfolio

Now that you understand the seven types of capital that make up your life, it's time to evaluate your own assets. Investing Your Life for maximum returns requires building your own Life Portfolio through a five-step process:

1. **Take Stock** of your life
2. Understand your **Money Supply**
3. Perform **Research** on options
4. Set **Price Targets**
5. Compare to **Benchmarks**

These steps should look familiar to anyone who has built a financial portfolio. You may want to read through the entire process before taking any specific action. If you are energized and want to begin immediately, go for it! Whether you decide to tackle these steps now or later, it's important to approach this work with your mind relaxed and calm, when you aren't preoccupied with a late work project or finding a ride for your daughter to band practice. Give yourself permission to intentionally set your worries aside for a few minutes, investing your time so you can be fully present throughout this process.

Before we begin, take a guess: On a scale from 1–10, what is your level of Living Fully today? "Living Fully" can be difficult to understand at first, especially in terms of what it means to you. It will be interesting to evaluate your feelings now and at the end of the process, so take a minute and give yourself a score.

Take Stock

Much like the map at a shopping mall with an arrow that says, "You are here," it's as important to know where you're starting from as it is to know your destination. We must examine where we are right now before the journey can really begin. You have already begun the process of Taking Stock in Chapter Seven, through the Values Discovery Questionnaire. Knowing your top values is a critical foundation for building your Life Portfolio. Literally every choice you make about both your money and your life should be built on those values.

I've often referred to the intersection of money and life as the "wealth exchange," similar to the New York Stock Exchange, where investments are traded. The wealth exchange is a place where money comes into contact with life: work, health, play, learning, relationships, and purpose.

The first step in understanding where you are today is taking the Living Fully Audit.

As you consider your life right now, rate your level of fulfillment and satisfaction in each category by circling or shading a 1, 2, or 3 (Low, Moderate, or High satisfaction). Try not to overthink your answers—just respond with whatever comes to your mind spontaneously.

After rating yourself in each of these categories, how would you summarize the overall level of fulfillment and satisfaction in your life today? Are your answers in many of the categories Low, Moderate, or High? Are

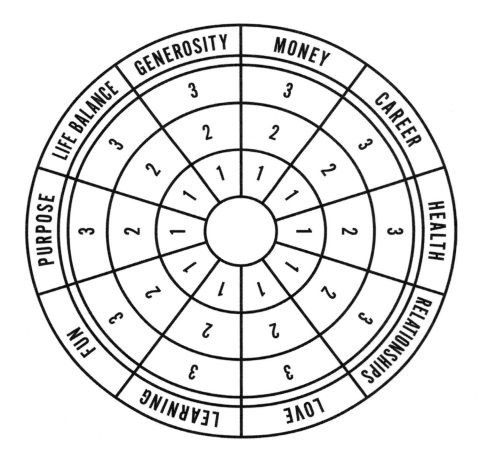

1=LOW   2=MODERATE   3=HIGH

Figure 9.1   Living Fully Audit

you feeling very fulfilled in certain categories and not at all satisfied in others? This is a valuable self-awareness exercise to highlight what is working for you and where potential problems may exist.

The shape of your wheel tells the story of your life at this moment. Often, we focus most of our time and energy on two or three categories, while other important aspects of "Living Fully" are neglected. You may find that only one or two categories in your assessment are rated "High" for satisfaction. Which "Low"- or "Moderate"-rated categories do you most want to improve? If Health has a "Low" satisfaction score for you right now, and you want to increase your overall fitness and wellness, is this a category you might want to invest in? If Love is at "Moderate" contentment and you want to experience more from an intimate relationship, perhaps this is an area you could focus on.

I want you to circle the top 1–3 categories that you are most drawn to. As we progress through the "Living Fully" framework and begin to build a Life Portfolio, keep these categories in mind as areas where you might invest more time and resources. A coach may be helpful in setting targets for improvement and giving you accountability through the process of change. As you experience improved results in these categories, you can always return to this exercise and find additional areas for improvement.

Resist becoming frustrated by your current circumstances—you may have more categories that are scored "Low" than you hoped for or expected. There are times when all facets of life are working well, spinning like an Indy race-car tire. In other seasons, your energy level is low, friendships are distant, and your financial life is causing a lot of anxiety. If that is the case, it's OK to accept this as your present reality. However, allow yourself to be curious: Why are you feeling this way about life?

As I shared in the story of my journey to live more fully (Chapter One), my career, life balance, and finding greater purpose were the areas I targeted in the early stages of discovery. I knew that I wasn't satisfied with my work situation, and I wanted a level of freedom and creativity that just wasn't available to me without starting my own company. My life felt out of balance, and I wanted to pump air into specific areas that needed attention, like investing in my relationship with my wife and kids and pursuing hobbies that interested me. I also wanted to really experience greater purpose in a daily way, as a faith or spiritual journey of sorts, and this felt super-risky.

Cami, an attendee at one of my "Investing Your Life" workshops, shared this about her experience "Taking Stock" of her life:

The Taking Stock section was super-meaningful to me . . . it made me slow down and reflect on where I'm at. For me, my 20s were spent pleasing others and trying to figure out who I want to be. Now, I'm in my 30s and have realized that life really is a journey and I don't have to have it all figured out. Things can change and I don't have to do what everyone else is doing or what they want me to do. I get to decide and choose, not everyone else. It was good to recognize that fear was what has been holding me back to this point, way more than I realized.

HERE ARE A FEW OTHER QUESTIONS TO CONSIDER AS YOU TAKE STOCK OF WHERE YOU ARE TODAY:

- Are you able to give yourself permission to live an amazing, abundant life? Does living a mediocre life feel safer?
- What stage of life are you in right now? What are the challenges and opportunities of this time and place?
- What are the really big things you want to experience, do, see, or create in your life?
- What is keeping you stuck, distracted, or living smaller than you desire?

Something to note: Not everyone is ready or wants to change things in life, and that's OK. I'm not here to shame or judge you for not taking action on a better life experience right now. You might feel that this initial step of introspection and awareness is all that you are capable of exploring at this time. It could also be that the pain points aren't severe enough to motivate you to change anything yet.

Where you are right now can be a zone of safety because it's what you know. In this position, you can know with high surety what life will deliver, even if you secretly hope for something better. As you take stock, my hope is that you will build momentum for future forward action, just like pulling back a rubber band before it snaps forward. Taking Stock is the fuel to ignite your momentum toward a more fulfilling and meaningful life.

Money Supply

The next important step in understanding and building your Life Portfolio is taking an honest and thorough look at your Money Supply. This step includes everything from evaluating the size and health of your financial base (cash, investments, real estate, debt, etc.), to calculating whether the financial formula for your life is sustainable. In other words, are your annual spending and lifestyle choices in line with your income sources? What are the investment and savings targets that will ensure your financial well-being into the future? You may have already started this process by calculating your financial "enoughness" in Chapter One.

If you already have a wealth advisory relationship in place, this is an exercise you can conduct with the help of your advisor. If you don't currently have an advisor, there are a variety of tools and resources available online to assist you (see Appendix), along with the questions posed at the end of this section.

The health of your Money Supply is important to your Life Portfolio because it represents a key energy source for achieving the things that matter most to you. It represents your level of financial confidence. Your money supply will amplify, magnify, and expand the boundaries of what's possible. Imagine that each of the components of your Life Portfolio is an individual stock: depending on your life choices, you can increase the investment allocation in the stocks that matter most to you. Your investments in these "life stocks" include your time, energy, and thought, but money also plays an important role here.

Your Money Supply is critical to Living Fully because it can be difficult to evaluate opportunities and enjoy other aspects of your life if money represents uncertainty and creates excess anxiety. When I ask you to dream about exciting alternatives in your life, you might not be able to fully engage in the conversation if you're distracted by money concerns, or spend the emotional energy needed without a clear sense of your financial footing. Like stepping into a swimming pool and not being sure where the bottom is, uncertainty about your Money Supply doesn't create the confidence needed to think big.

I was in a coaching discussion with a very successful doctor on transition decisions that he faced because of a health condition that almost killed him. He was much more sensitive to the quality of life he desired and how he wanted to spend his time than ever before. He wasn't terminally ill, but he had the motivation to live as though he were—only spending time on things that aligned with his most valued outcomes. (A result that we all might learn from, as everyone is "terminally ill" in actuality.) His kids were clearly number one on the priority list, and he was committed to being an active and present parent.

His career was a key part of his life satisfaction equation. He held a senior role at an internationally known medical center for many years, but he was ready for a change that might reignite his passion for medicine and allow him to serve in a fresh way. As we explored career alternatives, it was clear that the ideas we discussed were intriguing to him, but he was stuck emotionally. While he wanted to engage fully in the exercise, I could tell that something was holding him back.

My experience in similar situations has taught me that this is the point where it's important to clarify the financial situation. Understanding your Money Supply frees you to ponder life from a higher perch, with much less fear and uncertainty. We spent time calculating his level of financial independence in a variety of potential scenarios, giving him a sharper image of his Money Supply. He had been making assumptions about what was possible based on an inaccurate view through his financial binoculars. He was able to expand the scope of his thinking about what was possible once he had confidence that his Money Supply was sufficient for the future. It was as if I had given him permission to dream.

As discussed in Chapter Four, it's also important to understand the emotional impact that money has on your life choices, as well as how it amplifies, magnifies, and sometimes blurs your current reality and decision-making ability. The way you think about money leads to emotional impacts and directly influences your actions, behaviors, and decisions. Everyone has a relationship with money; it's either healthy, unhealthy, or you might be unaware that you even have one. Through understanding your level of abundance and stewardship, you can consciously recognize behavioral responses to money such as Contentment, Control, Concern, and Caution.

It's easy to jump to victimlike default responses with statements like, "If only I had more money, I would. . ." It's common to see people putting the expectations they have for a Life Portfolio on hold because of perceived or real lack of resources. While the level of your resources is relevant to making plans and exploring options, I would encourage you not to use your level of satisfaction (or dissatisfaction) with your Money Supply as an excuse to delay taking action. Remember, your money is a means to support and achieve important life outcomes, not the end in itself.

THE FOLLOWING QUESTIONS WILL PROVIDE ADDITIONAL POINTS OF ANALYSIS FOR YOUR MONEY SUPPLY:

- Do you find yourself living your life from a place of abundance or scarcity, and why?

- How much money represents "enough" for you? How do you define financial success? (Be honest and specific!)

- In what ways is money amplifying or detracting from your life, dreams, choices, confidence, and freedom?

- How would you describe your relationship to money? (Healthy, having a spat, victimized, etc.)

If you are still creating wealth and don't yet have the resources to fully fund your objectives, that's OK. Give yourself a break. Working with the resources that you have available now and being aware of how money influences you emotionally will give you plenty of ammo to begin the next step in creating your Life Portfolio: researching where meaning and purpose reside.

Research

Now that you know more about where you are now, the areas of your life that you want to focus on, and the health of your Money Supply, you need to know what lights the fire of your heart, what you care about, and the best options for investing your life's energy. Just as we thoroughly research stocks, mutual funds, and other investments before committing our capital, it is critical that we take the time to examine: "What's my life for?" The answers to this question will guide us as we decide how to invest our time, talents, energy, money, and other resources.

The core values discussed in Chapter Seven provide the starting point for any discussion about discovering your purpose and calling. In my experience, these values often leave clues found in our vocational or avocational work. Your work, whether for earned income or not, can be the vessel that brings your values into the daylight.

For Susan, a wealth creator employed at Amazon, work has always been something she valued highly. She loved the process of going after a challenge, working hard, and seeing results. Susan felt incredibly fulfilled by her accomplishments—being part of a team that invented and brought world-class products to market, building and leading talented teams, being a mentor to working moms. But as she recently celebrated her 40th birthday, other factors are taking priority.

"Now more than ever, I am motivated by work that fits best into my values, and my values center around my family, making connections in my community and nature, identifying and bringing out the best in people, exploring new challenges, experimenting and figuring out how to make things better for people, building new and exciting things, being present each day and trusting my gut to tell me how to work. In other words, how to create value in whatever I do."

Trevor is an uber-successful entrepreneur who started a technology company almost on a whim and monetized it over the past five years, to the point where he has more resources than he ever could have imagined. Because he doesn't need to work for an income anymore, he sits on several boards of companies, gives lots of time to philanthropic organizations, and is a great dad. All of this activity is wonderful, but it doesn't get him out of bed on Monday morning fired up with a passion for life. Trevor has struggled with a lack of calling, and he is unsure how to move forward. He has created a lot of busyness in his life that doesn't allow him time to slow down and really think about what would add joy, purpose, and meaning to his Life Portfolio.

I believe this is a place where wealth creators often get stuck—filling life up so completely that there isn't any room for thinking, let alone adding anything else to the equation of life. Learning to intentionally create space in your life and not feel pressure to fill the vacuum because of our discomfort is a great skill to develop. These open spaces are extremely valuable moments where reflection can occur. The author and speaker Bob Goff courageously quit his former law career in search of a higher calling. Now he routinely looks for things to quit in his life that have run their course or no longer serve their purpose, creating space for new opportunities to take shape.

It takes intentional due diligence and working through a process of discovery to understand your meaning and purpose in life. Much of this work is "inner work," and most of us haven't ever been taught how to do it, or we don't take the time because life is busy. For that reason, it can be uncomfortable at first. However, just as finding and investing in an undervalued stock can reap significant profits, so can taking the risk of exploring what truly brings you joy. Consider yourself a researcher mining for data about where purpose might be hiding.

When I initially worked through these questions myself, I remember how hard it was to uncover the answers. I needed the guidance of a coach who could listen to me process the various layers of my life and help orient my thinking, reflecting back what I was saying. Sometimes we need another person to hold up a mirror to our lives, allowing us to see things that we wouldn't be able to otherwise. An accountability partner can challenge us to keep digging so that we don't miss the plunder that lies just a few feet ahead of us, providing encouragement and permission to believe that we can experience something richer and more meaningful than what we have right now.

When I'm talking with a wealth creator, I know when we are hovering over a place of extreme passion and purpose in her life because her eyes twinkle, a smile comes to her face, and her whole body exudes energy that says, "This is important to me." When I see it, or feel it, I can often reflect back to this person what I'm witnessing—even the pitch and intensity of her voice increase. It's as if her soul has been exposed. It can feel embarrassing to be seen that way, but I believe we inherently know that these areas of our life are sacred.

If you have worked through the questions in Chapter Eight exploring your "Highest Calling," congratulations! You have already completed the foundational research necessary to build your Life Portfolio. If you have not yet invested the time and thought needed to explore your Highest Calling, use the following questions as a preliminary assessment, much like putting a finger in the air to gauge which direction the wind is blowing.

PONDER AND WRITE ABOUT THE FOLLOWING QUESTIONS:

- Money is not an end but a means—a means for achieving something of importance to you. What is important to you?
- What are the most important elements of work in your life, whether or not you are getting paid? Why do you work? What is your definition of work? How have you experienced personal fulfillment through work?
- What would you do if you knew you wouldn't fail?
- What activities do you do that make you completely lose track of time or bring out the best in you?

The answers to these questions, as well as the questions in Chapter Eight, should help you recognize the areas of your life that are the most fulfilling and exciting. Understanding where you find the most joy becomes the arrow on your personal compass, pointing you toward the places where you can provide the highest and most meaningful contribution.

Price Targets

When I was a stockbroker many years ago, I would cold-call potential investors and tell them the story of the investment I was pitching that day. I had 30–60 seconds to create interest in the company, and a big part of that sales process was highlighting how much money could be earned—in other words, the trajectory they could expect from this investment. *Mr. and Mrs. Smith, our analysts have a "buy" rating on this stock because we believe it will generate a return of 35 percent over the next 12–18 months based on our research.*

Understanding the price target for a stock is important in defining expectations; otherwise, you won't know if it has been a good investment. Similarly, I want you to consciously choose targets for your life (what I refer to as "ideal outcomes"). There's an old saying that goes, "If you don't know where you're going, any road will get you there." In financial portfolios, when we know our return objectives, we are able to pick appropriate investments to achieve those expectations. The same applies to your Life Portfolio: Picking your target will help you get on the road to your desired destination. The by-product of reaching our ideal outcome is joy, peace, and fulfillment—similar to reaching a price target for a stock and profiting on our investment.

I had lunch recently with Mark, a wealth creator who had left a successful career at Starbucks with a gob of money earned over a long career. I asked him, "Are you living fully now?" His explosive response was "Hell the f***, no!"

"Why not?" I asked. He understood intellectually how good his life was, but viscerally, he was not enjoying the ride. Despite the fact that he had plenty of money to secure his family's financial future, Mark continued to feel great anxiety in his life and a lack of abundance, even as the monetary value of his portfolio continued to rise. He had lost faith in both for-profit and not-for-profit organizations, and he was wrestling with an extremely pessimistic belief that life is meaningless. In previous conversations, Mark had stated that his ideal outcome was time freedom, but now having achieved it in abundance, there wasn't a target for his life. This left him feeling lost, untethered to any purpose or meaning.

Several years ago, I was leading a session at my church's change group for men called Genesis Process. One of the questions in the curriculum of this program was helpful to me in setting a target for my future life. It asked, "If you could do anything using your God-given gifts that would bring you joy and fulfillment, what would you do?" I listed several things, including thought leadership through writing and speaking about the challenges and opportunities at the intersection of money and life; coaching high-achieving, wealth-creating couples to find a deeper sense of meaning and purpose; working with my wife to establish a marriage and relationship retreat and renewal center in a cool location; and facilitating and supporting the men in my Genesis Change program. At the time, that felt like a daunting but exciting list of objectives, and when I cracked open that old workbook recently, I was pleasantly surprised to see that I was on track to accomplishing most, if not all, of these items. There is great power in setting clear and intentional objectives—it's fascinating to see how my life has been drawn to these targets almost unconsciously.

I don't believe that we intentionally aim for targets that are too low, but like Mark, we will know when we haven't aimed high enough. We will feel frustration that we aren't experiencing more in life and regret that we wasted precious time on stocks that were too safe or didn't have much upside.

PONDER AND WRITE ABOUT THE FOLLOWING QUESTIONS:

- What does success mean to you? (Think personally, professionally, financially . . .) Are you able to quantify the expected return?
- Assuming that you have all the money you would need and you knew that you would succeed, what would you do differently in your life? (Think relationships, work, community, health, experiences, spirituality . . .)

- Look into the future 5 or 10 years from now. Imagine that we are sitting together having a cup of coffee, and you begin to tell me how wonderful your life is. What specifically is happening that makes you feel that way?
- Describe your fondest hope for the future. Does this vision for your future scare you at all? If not, is this vision big enough or exciting enough?

Benchmarks

The financial markets are uncertain, and new information presents itself that challenges our original assumptions about a certain investment or the way we allocate our resources. Evaluating your investment portfolio against a benchmark or index broadens your perspective and improves the ability to make midcourse corrections as needed. For example, if one of your stocks is up 5 percent, but the overall U.S. stock market has returned 15 percent during the same period of time, you can benchmark and compare that result, deciding whether you want to stick with that stock or make a change.

Benchmarks are a critical measuring tool to understand the various components of your Life Portfolio, recognizing which of your life stocks needs greater attention or even major changes, to increase your rate of return on a life fully lived. The following assessment provides a way to measure which assets in your Life Portfolio are performing well and which may be underperforming:

My Life Portfolio Assessment

Review the various types of capital that make up your own Life Portfolio. Consider where you are right now, and where you would like to be as you "invest" each area of your life resources. Then complete the My Life Portfolio Assessment.

Financial Capital (Money)—Confidence, freedom, peace of mind, simplicity, generosity, contentment, values alignment, impact

Vocational Capital (Work)—Meaningful contribution, high emotional engagement, potential to win, talent and skills alignment, personal achievement, passion about mission and vision

Social Capital (Relationships)—Family, friends, community, connections, influence

Experiential Capital (Play)— Fun, hobbies, interests, adventure, travel, pure enjoyment

Physiological Capital (Health)—Physical and emotional health, fitness, gratitude, happiness, life satisfaction, positive energy

Intellectual Capital (Mind)—Continuous learning, curiosity, personal growth and development, consciousness, abundance

Spiritual Capital (Purpose)—Faith, higher power, deeply held beliefs, core values, meaning of life, legacy

MY LIFE PORTFOLIO
Take a few minutes to contemplate and answer the following questions, grading yourself on a 1–10 scale (1 is low, 10 is high):

As you look at your money overall, and without comparing yourself to anyone else, what grade would you give your Financial Capital right now?

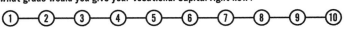

As you look at your work overall, and without comparing yourself to anyone else, what grade would you give your Vocational Capital right now?

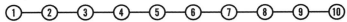

As you look at your positive relationships overall, and without comparing yourself to anyone else, what grade would you give your Social Capital right now?

As you look at your experiences and enjoyment of life, and without comparing yourself to anyone else, what grade would you give your Experiential Capital right now?

As you look at your health, and without comparing yourself to anyone else, what grade would you give your Physiological Capital right now?

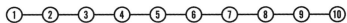

As you look at your mind and intellect, and without comparing yourself to anyone else, what grade would you give your Intellectual Capital right now?

As you look at your purpose and spirit, and without comparing yourself to anyone else, what grade would you give your Spiritual Capital right now?

Why did you give yourself those grades?
What is one thing you could do to improve the grade in each area?

Figure 9.2   My Life Portfolio Assessment

How do you feel about your score on each type of life capital? Were there any surprises? By looking at your score for each stock in your portfolio and adding up the total, you can get a sense of which stocks are performing well and the overall health of your Life Portfolio. You'll also quickly see which parts of your life might need more attention.

Now take a moment to look back at the Values Discovery Questionnaire in Chapter Seven—what were the five most important values you wrote down? Also look back at the Price Targets questions earlier in this chapter, and think about your vision for an ideal future. Are there areas of cross-over between your most important values, things you want to achieve in your ideal future, and a particular life capital that will help you realize your ideal outcomes?

For example, say the grade that you gave your Physiological Capital stock is 6 out of 10. You notice that this area shows up as one of your top values, and your ideal outcome is to run a marathon in the next year—this would be a good place to focus by writing down one or two things you could do to improve your grade. It might not be reasonable to shoot for a 10 in that category, but maybe you would like to be an 8 within the next year. Ask yourself: "What actions would I need to take over the next year to move from a 6 to an 8?"

You can do this review with each of the stocks in your portfolio where you don't feel the score is where you want it to be. You may feel that certain stocks are performing very well—maybe your Vocational Capital score is 8, and you are happy with that outcome. There will be areas where you don't want or need to make any adjustments at this time, and that is OK.

To evaluate your overall Life Portfolio, add up the scores for each of the stocks. The maximum score is 70 (seven stocks, at 10 points each), and let's say your total is 49. As a percentage, that's 70 percent, or a C– grade for your Life Portfolio as a whole. How does that make you feel? This is gut-check time because you may or may not want to put in the work to achieve a higher score. My hope is that you will want more for your life, and thanks to these exercises, you will see what is possible. If you do want a better return on life, how about setting a target to invest more in one or two categories? Aiming for an A+ on your Life Portfolio score in the long term is great—what would you have to do to move yourself in that direction? Evaluate your ideas and progress against your ideal outcomes as the ultimate destination, using this tool as the compass to confirm that you are right on course.

To give you an idea of how these tools and ideas might play out in your life, let's follow the journey of an aspiring wealth creator through the Life Portfolio process. Ashley is a 31-year-old wealth creator from Minneapolis who was feeling stuck in her career, her finances, and her relationships. She felt disappointed that her life seemed fixed on a lower trajectory than she had hoped for. Resentment and anger toward herself and others were building: Ashley was living a fear-based life of scarcity, weighed down in part by the financial and emotional impacts of a husband who had difficulty holding down a job and contributing meaningfully to their future, while she soldiered on alone, working her tail off chasing career and financial success. She experienced what she referred to as "monkeys on her back" from taking care of everyone else around her, at home and at work, with her needs always coming in second.

Ashley had grown up in a home where money was a stressful subject. Her parents did not model a healthy relationship with money, and she grew up with messages like "You better have a damn good reason if you want money for anything special." For Ashley, money was equated with financial and emotional security and stability, and her game plan had been to marry into money to eliminate her fears around not having enough.

Unsurprisingly, Ashley's relationship with money is complicated, with lots of emotional tentacles connected to her desire to be frugal, worry about her ability to save enough, and constant indecision about money for fear of making a bad choice. She would frequently overthink and overanalyze financial opportunities, which led to feelings of resentment, especially when meaningful experiences were missed in favor of cheap alternatives, justified in the name of sacrifice. Her controlling and security-based decisions contrasted with the practical reality that she was accumulating wealth rapidly through a start-up business she was involved in as a side hustle.

As Ashley began her journey of self-discovery and reflection, embarking on the inner work discussed in Chapters Seven, Eight, and Nine, she had a keen desire to be more open with her life and her money. She realized that she had to stop trying to control everything and everyone. She told me that once she decided to go inward to understand, heal, and change, she experienced an unquenchable determination and fire to see the process through. She was uncovering and embracing who she was created to be, and discovering how she wanted to orient her life for maximum meaning and purpose. She was no longer willing to settle for anything less than connecting her gifts of presence, listening, intuition, and encouragement to her entrepreneurial and fighter spirit. Ashley poignantly summarized her purpose as "helping women stand in their truth, and to be confident in that truth."

She started to see visions of a future that excited but also scared her. Ashley wanted to build her own business, be her own boss, and call the shots. The business she dreamed of was something designed to help and empower women, which incorporated a charitable element into the business plan. In addition, she had a strong desire to coach and mentor young women in their early 20s, offering the kind of support that she had desperately needed and lacked at that age. Her ideal future also included becoming a mom and creating a network of healthy and strong friend and family relationships.

This ideal outcome felt right, and appropriately risky: It would require her to be more vulnerable and push her to grow in new ways, and it had financial implications because she would be "throwing away" a guaranteed six-figure salary for the unknown territory of entrepreneurship. Achieving clarity about what she most wanted for her future created a high level of anabolic energy for Ashley in a way that she had never experienced before.

Ashley's view of the future has changed dramatically through the process of analyzing and building her Life Portfolio: Now anything is possible, where there were nothing but limits and constraints before. She recognizes her own capability to change and evolve, to think bigger about her future, and to stop worrying what others think of her and her choices. Ashley wants to live fully in each moment, showing up as her authentic self. With gratitude for this newfound clarity around her life, she is experiencing joy, confidence, and excitement about what lies ahead.

Investing Your Life

Through the Investing Your Life framework and the My Life Portfolio Assessment, you are now equipped to understand who you are, your current life circumstances, the future you are seeking, the influence and health of your money, and the most meaningful and impactful path for your journey ahead. Unfortunately, as most have learned or will soon learn, our best-laid plans can dramatically change because the unexpected happens to each of us.

Imagine that you're on a sailing excursion—you have charted a specific course, but shifting winds and a strong current throw the bow of your boat off course, requiring you to adjust your sails and tack. A compass is a very useful instrument when sailing because it points the way to get back on track. Likewise, the My Life Portfolio assessment is a critical tool, showing you where you are on the map of your life's journey and helping you chart a course to your ideal outcome for the future.

As you come to understand how the seven types of life capital are working in your life, you can make adjustments and balance your Life Portfolio. Perhaps there are areas where you need to increase your investment, or areas where you are overinvested in terms of your time and energy. It may be helpful to retake the My Life Portfolio Assessment every 6 or 12 months to accurately evaluate how your Life Portfolio is performing.

I believe that the life investment game is played over the long term, just like sound investment strategy. As in the financial markets, if you follow the crowd's opinions, they are frequently wrong. Are you too focused on the short term, or influenced by the opinions of others when it comes to building your Life Portfolio? Remember to listen to your inner voice, look at the bigger picture of your life, and hold firm to your convictions.

Maximizing your returns may also require taking some risks. What is the return you are expecting from your Life Portfolio? Have you set your sights too low? Are you being too conservative and missing out on the growth and returns that benefit those who take more risk? Big money is patient and stays invested for the long run to compound and work in ways that short-term expectations can't match. I want my life to compound and be maximized over the long term. I'm playing the long game.

Pablo Picasso said, "The meaning of life is to find your gift. The purpose of life is to give it away." I would add that the purpose of life is to invest your gift so that it can be enjoyed by many. All of life is a gift, not just our money. Every part of our Life Portfolio has gifts for the wealth creator. How we utilize the gifts during our lifetime will quantify the return we can experience. I don't think you were given these gifts to keep them hidden or to hoard them for your own exclusive benefit and enjoyment. I believe that God provided you with these gifts for a purpose. You have a contribution to make in the world that is unique and important.

What steps will you take to invest your life for maximum returns?

Afterword: Making the All-Star Team

Congratulations on finishing *The Wealth Creator's Playbook*! You now have a game plan for your journey to Living Fully, and the knowledge and framework to invest your life for maximum returns.

Making the All-Star team in Little League is the coolest thing for a 10- or 11-year-old. Coaching one of those teams is an experience I'll never forget. Our team of 10-year-olds fought their way through the losers bracket to reach the finals, needing to win twice to advance to the state tournament. We won the first and lost the second game by only one run in a heartbreaker. It was as exciting and dramatic an experience as any professional game I've seen. I will never forget the pure joy in the eyes of those boys proudly running onto the diamond in their new blue-and-red uniforms, with pennant flags flying, umpires in their blues, and fans surrounding the field. They were walking on water.

I challenge you to be an All-Star investor in life and money by putting the information that you've gained from this book into action—evaluate your Life Portfolio and look for opportunities to improve your return. As a wealth creator, you have advantages that others can only dream of, and you have a responsibility to steward those resources well. There are no do-overs in baseball or in life, so start making the most of the time and opportunities that you've been granted. Don't accept a backup role, standing on the sidelines doing nothing, placing this book on your actual or virtual bookshelf as a trophy of your latest reading conquest. There are no practice games in life, only the regular season. My hope is that the pages of this Playbook are dog-eared and highlighted, with notes scribbled in the margins, and your soul wants to experience change, possibly even transformation.

I've learned through facilitating change workshops for many years that one of the biggest impediments in taking action toward any kind of change is usually ourselves. If it were easy to change, we would have done it by now, and we can often trick ourselves into believing that change will happen if we just give it enough time. Often, we devise a defense that requires no real commitment or responsibility on our part. In fact, many times we don't want to experience a better return on life because we just plain don't want to put in the work. If that is you, I can't help you. This game favors anyone who has the drive to be a starter on the team: When you are ready to take on that challenge, I'm here to coach you.

Sometimes our life circumstances can feel overwhelming, and we can get stuck, scared, and unsure about where to start. By breaking big issues into small and digestible action steps, it's easier to get started, see positive movement forward, and not get frustrated by lack of progress. Start with one or two areas in your Life Portfolio that you want to focus on, or simply commit to working through the Research step in the Investing Your Life process. Whatever you choose to do, the step should be realistic and have a level of difficulty that introduces a sense of challenge or risk to the equation; otherwise, you may not achieve a meaningful return.

When I ask the groups I facilitate through this process to decide on an action step that moves them toward their desired outcomes, I often get watered-down responses that might sound like movement but are just trivial attempts. When I challenge them to take on something more, the response is often, "Oh, no, that would be risky" or "It would scare the heck out of me if I did that!" That's when I know we're in the ballpark of real change.

The other reason why progress stalls is lack of intentional support and accountability. Most of us don't have a community where we can be heard and validated, be encouraged to keep going, be held accountable to our objectives, learn from others, and be inspired to target a grander vision and outcome for our lives. Often, the people I talk to say that they don't have relationships where they can be honest and vulnerable about their life, sharing struggles and dreams, worries and joys. Because money is such a taboo subject in our culture and has an isolating influence, it can be difficult to talk openly with anyone about your money history, money EQ, and how money is affecting your ideal outcomes. For this reason, I've created a virtual community for current and aspiring wealth creators to find inspiration, tools, resources, and an engaged group of like-minded people who are serious about financial returns but, more important, are seeking a truly wealthy life. To find out more about the Living Fully Community

and the resources available to you, please visit my website at www
.jcchristianson.com.

I believe it's possible for you to have it all, and I hope that now you can
see it, too. Go make it happen, because I can't imagine an objective more
important than what we were created for: life fully lived!

Living Fully,
John

Appendix: Financial Tools and Resources

Financial Planning Tools—
  SEC/FINRA (www.investor.gov)
  Vanguard Retirement (www.retirementplans.vanguard.com)
  Financial Mentor (www.financialmentor.com)
  SmartAsset (www.smartasset.com)
Asset Allocation and Portfolio Management—
  Wealthfront (www.wealthfront.com)
  Betterment (www.betterment.com)
  Personal Capital (www.personalcapital.com)
  Vanguard (www.personal.vanguard.com)
  Portfolio Visualizer (www.portfoliovisualizer.com)
  Portfolio Charts (www.portfoliocharts.com)
Financial Industry Organizations—
  Certified Financial Planner (www.cfp.net)
  Chartered Financial Analyst (www.cfainstitute.org)
  U.S. Securities and Exchange Commission (SEC) (www.investor.gov)
Budgeting/Bill Pay—Mint (www.mint.com)
Financial Products Review—NerdWallet (www.nerdwallet.com)
Alternative Investments Primer—World Economic Forum (www.weforum.org /reports)

Notes

1. Charlotte Wold, "The Number of Millionaires Continues to Increase," *Investopedia,* April 26, 2018; accessed July 9, 2018, from http://www.investopedia.com/news/number-millionaires-continues-increase/.

2. Ibid.

3. David M. Buss, "The Evolution of Happiness," *American Psychologist,* 55 (2000):15–23.

4. David G. Myers, "The Funds, Friends, and Faith of Happy People," *American Psychologist,* 55 (2000): 56–67 (italics in original).

5. Mihaly Csikszentmihalyi, "If We Are So Rich, Why Aren't We Happy?" *American Psychologist,* 54 (1999): 821–827.

6. Ric Edelman, "Why So Many Lottery Winners Go Broke," *Fortune,* January 15, 2016; accessed June 20, 2018, from http://fortune.com/2016/01/15/powerball-lottery-winners/.

7. Juliet B. Schor, *The Overspent American: Why We Want What We Don't Need* (New York: HarperCollins, 1999).

8. Suniya S. Luthar, "The Culture of Affluence: Psychological Costs of Material Wealth," *Child Development,* 74 (2003): 1581–1593; accessed June 23, 2018, from https://www.ncbi.nlm.nih.gov/pmc/articles/PMC1950124/.

9. Heather Bowen Ray, "Talking About Success and Stress with Brené Brown," *Thrive Global,* January 3, 2017; accessed June 11, 2018, from https://journal.thriveglobal.com/talking-about-success-and-stress-with-brené-brown-aa56855300fb.

10. Belinda Luscombe, "Do We Need $75,000 a Year to be Happy?" *Time,* September 6, 2010; accessed July 2, 2018, from http://content.time.com/time/magazine/article/0,9171,2019628,00.html.

11. Rudiger Sturm, "Jim Carrey: There Is No Me," *The Talks,* January 17, 2018; accessed August 3, 2018, from http://the-talks.com/interview/jim-carrey/.

12. Kristen Powers, "Americans Are Depressed and Suicidal Because There Is Something Wrong with Our Culture," *USA Today,* June 9, 2018; accessed August 10, 2018, from https://www.usatoday.com/story/opinion/2018/06/09/kate-spade-suicide-anthony-bourdain-depression-culture-success-column/687388002/.

13. Eventbrite, "The Experience Movement Research Report: How Millennials Are Bridging Cultural & Political Divides Offline"; accessed August 3, 2018, from https://www.eventbrite.com/l/millennialsreport-2017/.

14. DTTL Global Brand and Communications, "Mind the Gaps: The 2015 Deloitte Millennial Survey, Executive Summary," Deloitte, accessed July 19, 2018, from https://www2.deloitte.com/content/dam/Deloitte/global/Documents/About -Deloitte/gx-wef-2015-millennial-survey-executivesummary.pdf.

15. Christian Smith and Hilary Davidson, *The Paradox of Generosity* (New York: Oxford University Press, 2014).

16. Credit Suisse Research Institute, *Global Wealth Report 2017,* November 2017; accessed June 10, 2018, from http://publications.credit-suisse .com/index.cfm/publikationen-shop/research-institute/global-wealth-report -2017-en/.

17. Suniya S. Luthar, "The Culture of Affluence: Psychological Costs of Material Wealth," *Child Development,* 74 (2003): 1581–1593; accessed June 23, 2018, from https://www.ncbi.nlm.nih.gov/pmc/articles/PMC1950124/.

18. Ibid.

19. Ibid.

20. Paul K. Piff, Daniel M. Stancato, Stéphane Côté, Rodolfo Mendoza-Denton, and Dacher Keltner, "Higher Social Class Predicts Increased Unethical Behavior," PNAS, March 13, 2012; accessed June 18, 2018, from http://www.pnas.org/content /109/11/4086.full.

21. Ibid.

22. Jennifer E. Stellar, Vida M. Manzo, Michael W. Kraus, and Dacher Keltner, "Compassion and Class: Socioeconomic Factors Predict Compassionate Responding," *Emotion,* 12 (2012): 449–459.

23. "Statistics on U.S. Generosity," *The Philanthropy Roundtable,* accessed September 3, 2018 from https://www.philanthropyroundtable.org/almanac/statistics /u.s.-generosity.

24. Robert Powell, "Honoring the Man Who Forever Changed the Financial Planning Profession," *Marketwatch,* May 9, 2017; accessed August 1, 2018, from https://www.marketwatch.com/story/honoring-the-man-who-forever-changed -the-financial-planning-profession-2017-05-19.

25. "2016 Global Sustainable Investment Review," Global Sustainable Investment Alliance, 2017, accessed August 11, 2018 from https://www.ussif.org/files /Publications/GSIA_Review2016.pdf.

26. Morgan Stanley Institute for Sustainable Investing, "Sustainable Signals: New Data from the Individual Investor (Executive Summary)," August 7, 2017; accessed September 4, 2018, from https://www.morganstanley.com/pub/content /dam/msdotcom/ideas/sustainable-signals/pdf/Sustainable_Signals_Whitepaper .pdf.

27. Scorpio Partnership and Factset, "HNWI's Vision for the Wealth Management Industry in the Information Age," July 26, 2016; accessed August 29, 2018,

from https://msenterprise.global.ssl.fastly.net/wordpress/2017/07/Facset-The-Culture -Challenge_final-in-Wealth-Mgmt.pdf.

28. Alex Daniels, "As Wealthy Give Smaller Share of Income, Middle Class Digs Deeper," *The Chronicle of Philanthropy,* October 5, 2014; accessed September 3, 2018, from https://www.philanthropy.com/article/As-Wealthy-Give-Smaller-Share /152481.

29. Luke Iorio, "Breaking Down Energy: What You Need to Know as a Coach, Leader, Educator (or Human Being!)," *iPec Coaching* blog; accessed September 3, 2018, from https://ipeccoaching.com/breaking-down-energy/.

30. Lynne Twist, *The Soul of Money: Transforming Your Relationship with Money and Life* (New York: W.W. Norton & Company, 2017).

31. Joel Solomon, *The Clean Money Revolution* (Canada: New Society Publishers, 2017).

32. Adrian Furnham, "Watching the Money Go-Round," *Business Strategy Review,* 13(1) (2002): 67.

33. K-State News, "Researcher Finds Correlation Between Financial Arguments, Decreased Relationship Satisfaction," July 12, 2013; accessed July 30, 2018, from http://www.k-state.edu/media/newsreleases/jul13/predictingdivorce 71113.html.

34. Joan D. Atwood, "Couples and Money: The Last Taboo," *American Journal of Family Therapy,* 40 (2012): 1; accessed June 19, 2018, from doi:10.1080/01926 187.2011.600674.

35. "Poll: How Husbands and Wives Really Feel About Their Finances," *Money,* June 1, 2014; accessed July 30, 2018, from http://time.com/money/2800576/love -money-by-the-numbers/.

36. Gary Rivlin, "In Silicon Valley, Millionaires Who Don't Feel Rich," *The New York Times,* August 5, 2007, accessed July 10, 2018, https://www.nytimes.com/2007 /08/05/technology/05rich.html.

37. Chris Taylor, "The Last Taboo: Why Nobody Talks About Money," *Reuters,* March 27, 2014; accessed June 20, 2018, from https://www.reuters.com/article/us -money-conversation/the-last-taboo-why-nobody-talks-about-money-idUSBRE A2Q1UN20140327.

38. Amy Novotney, "Money Can't Buy Happiness," *Monitor on Psychology,* 43 (2012): 24.

39. Dan Baker and Cameron Stauth, *What Happy People Know: How the New Science of Happiness Can Change Your Life for the Better* (New York: St Martins Griffin, 2004).

40. Missy Sullivan, "Lost Inheritance," *Wall Street Journal,* March 8, 2013; accessed July 26, 2018, from https://www.wsj.com/articles/SB100014241278873 24662404578334663271139552.

41. Chris Taylor, "70% of Rich Families Lose Their Wealth by the Second Generation," *Time,* June 17, 2015; accessed July 30, 2018, from http://time.com /money/3925308/rich-families-lose-wealth/.

42. Emmie Martin, "7 Billionaires Who Won't Leave Their Fortunes to Their Kids," *CNBC,* July 6, 2017; accessed August 31, 2018, from https://www.cnbc .com/2017/07/06/billionaires-who-wont-leave-their-fortunes-to-their-kids.html.

43. C. Northcote Parkinson, "Parkinson's Law," *The Economist,* November 19, 1955; accessed July 31, 2018, from https://www.economist.com/news/1955/11 /19/parkinsons-law.

44. Sullivan, "Lost Inheritance."

Index

About the Author

John Christianson is founder and CEO of Highland Private Wealth Management, a boutique financial life management company in Bellevue, Washington. For more than 25 years, John has managed the financial lives of some of the most successful wealth creators in the country, including executives at Amazon, Microsoft, Starbucks, Nike, and Facebook, and he has acquired unique insights into the challenges and opportunities for wealth creators. John is the host and creator of *The Wealth Confidant* podcast. He is a CFA charterholder, a CPA–Inactive, and a certified professional coach with the International Coach Federation.

Connect with John

I'm passionate about helping you invest your life for maximum returns. If you have any questions or want to connect, please email me at john@jcchristianson.com.

To access the latest episodes of *The Wealth Confidant* podcast, and other tools and resources for a truly wealthy life, please visit my website at www.jcchristianson.com. Feel free to follow me on LinkedIn, Facebook, Instagram, and Twitter (@jcchristianson).

I offer wealth and life coaching for individuals and couples, speak to groups and organizations on how to live fully, and teach "Investing Your Life" workshops. For more information or to schedule a speaking engagement, sign up for a workshop, or book a coaching session, please email me or visit my website.